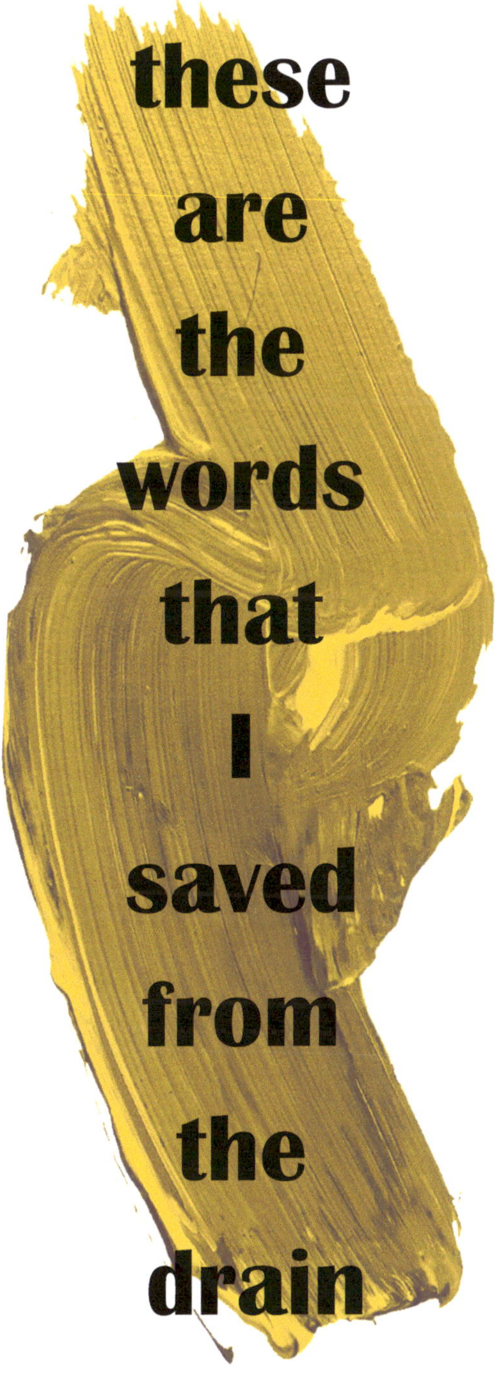

these are the words that I saved from the drain

poems by Dane Schneider

art by Kerri O'Halloran

these are the words that I saved from the drain

Poems by Dane Schneider
Artwork by Kerri O'Halloran

Published by: Dane Schneider and Kerri O’Halloran
Cover Design: Kerri O’Halloran
Portrait Photography: Kylee Leonetti
Artwork Photography: Kerri O’Halloran and Matthew Broadbent

A CIP record for this book is available from the Library of Congress Cataloging-in-Publication Data

ISBN-978-1-7378015-1-1

Printed in USA

Contents

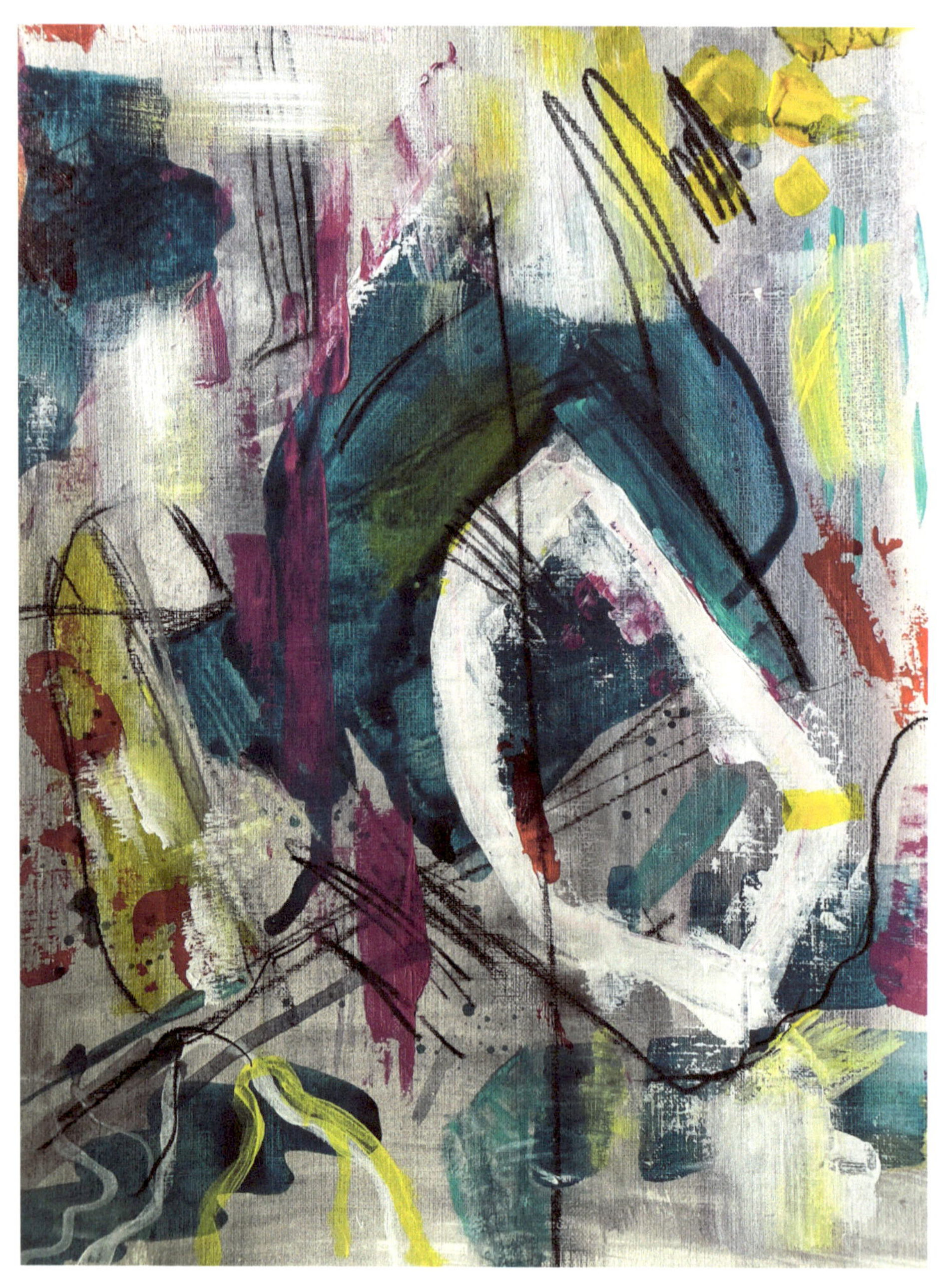

shame

there's
no
shame
in
solitude

but
there's
plenty
of
solitude

in
shame

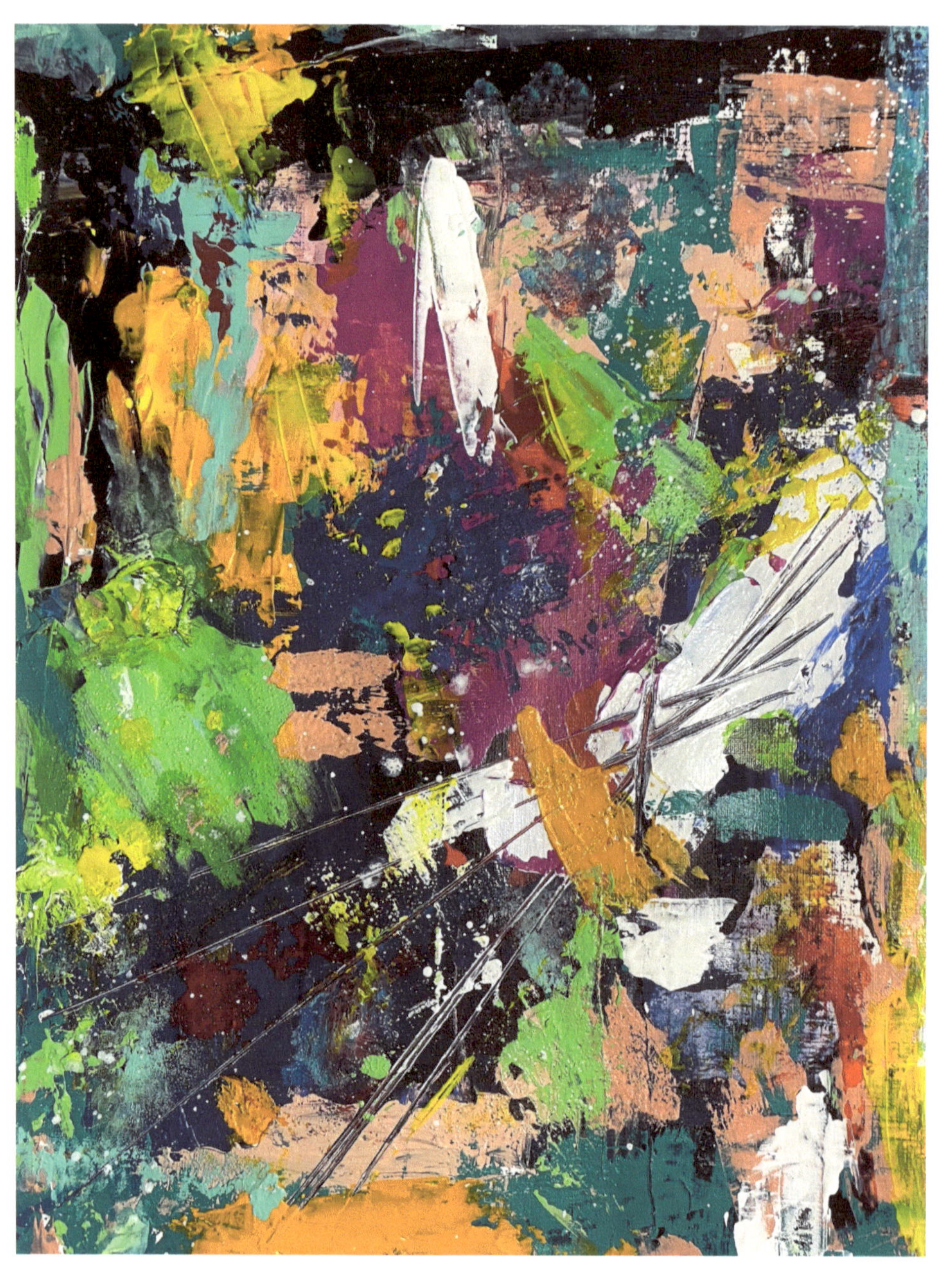

my body is a shape when it should be a feeling

sure I'm driving this thing and my name is on the registration
but it only ever felt like mine by designation
I'm just renting this body
it belongs to the mirrors the fears and the scales
but not me
it belongs to the nicknames the hidden and not so hidden shames
but not me
it belongs to overeating and anxieties of every variety
but not me
my body never even belonged to the present
always defined by what it had been or what it could be
never what it is
these hands
these eyes
this heart
I own the individual components
but when combined they are not mine
I lose all claims to ownership
my body is a shape when it should be a feeling
my body is a tool I use to hammer and screw
but never to mend
it's too ugly for that
I even cover it up at the beach
and sometimes recoil when touched
looking at old photos of myself
I almost get a sense of bereavement
if it felt like I owned this body
I wouldn't feel so inclined to leave it

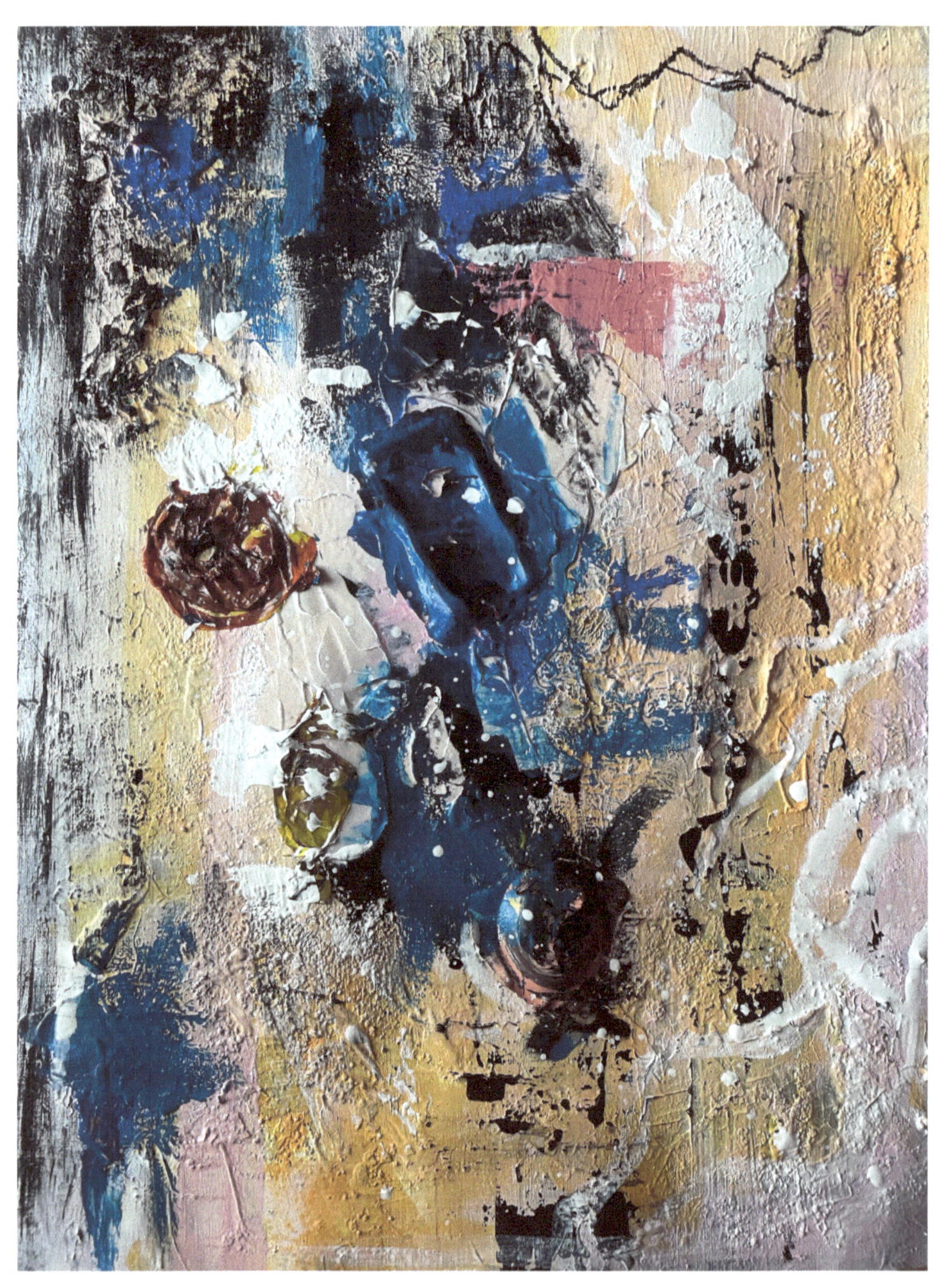

carnivorous

these
thoughts
are
carnivorous
and
they've
picked
up
my
scent

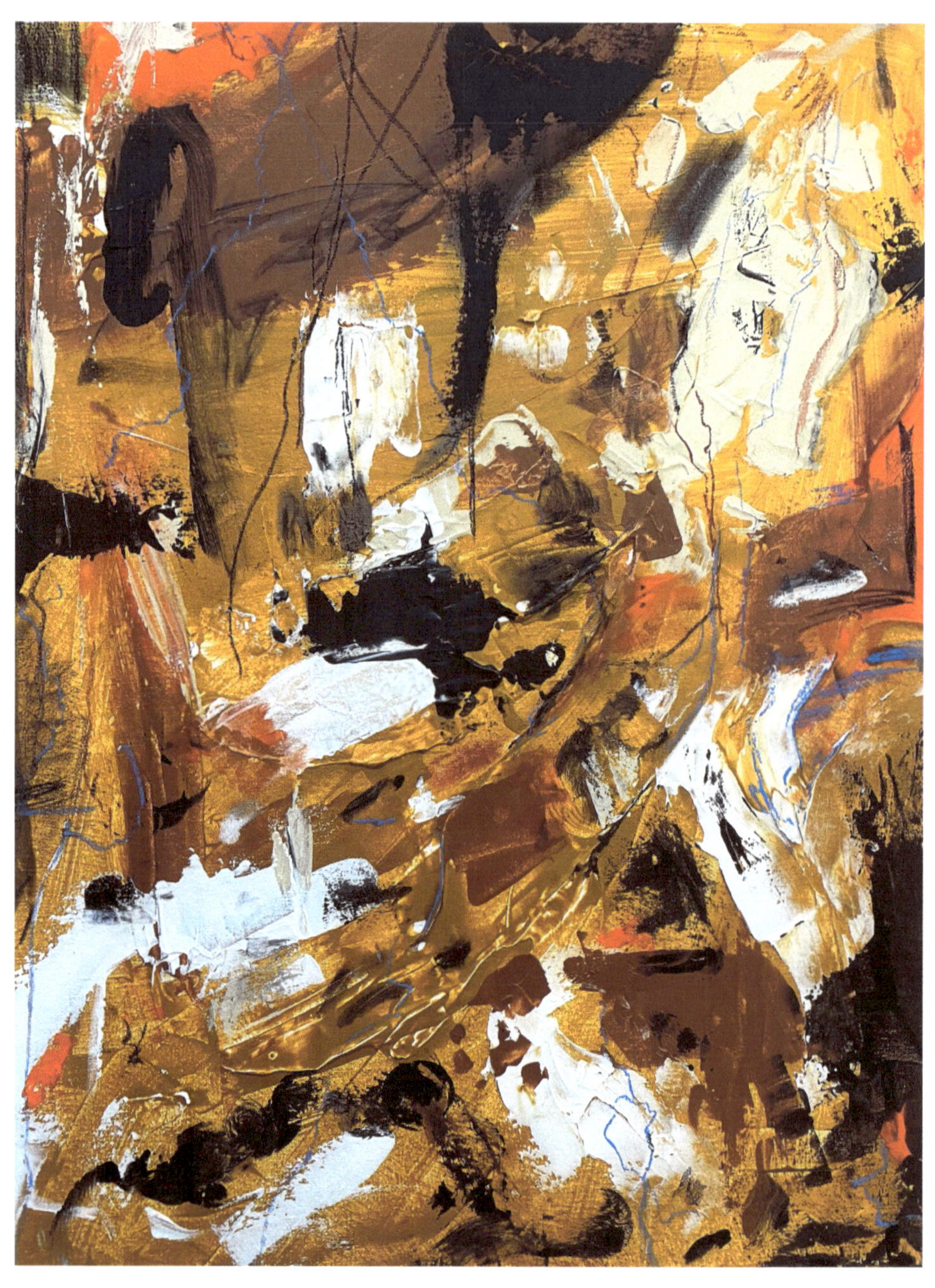

I am

I am expired poison
I am a squeaky hearse
I am a dial tone that's breaking up
I am a dream stuck in reverse
I am the future flipped over a curb
I am the dustpan without the broom
I am the television edit
I am the aura of a waiting room
I am the illusion of distance
I am decadence decayed
I am a pair of frayed sheets
I am everything that keeps you dismayed

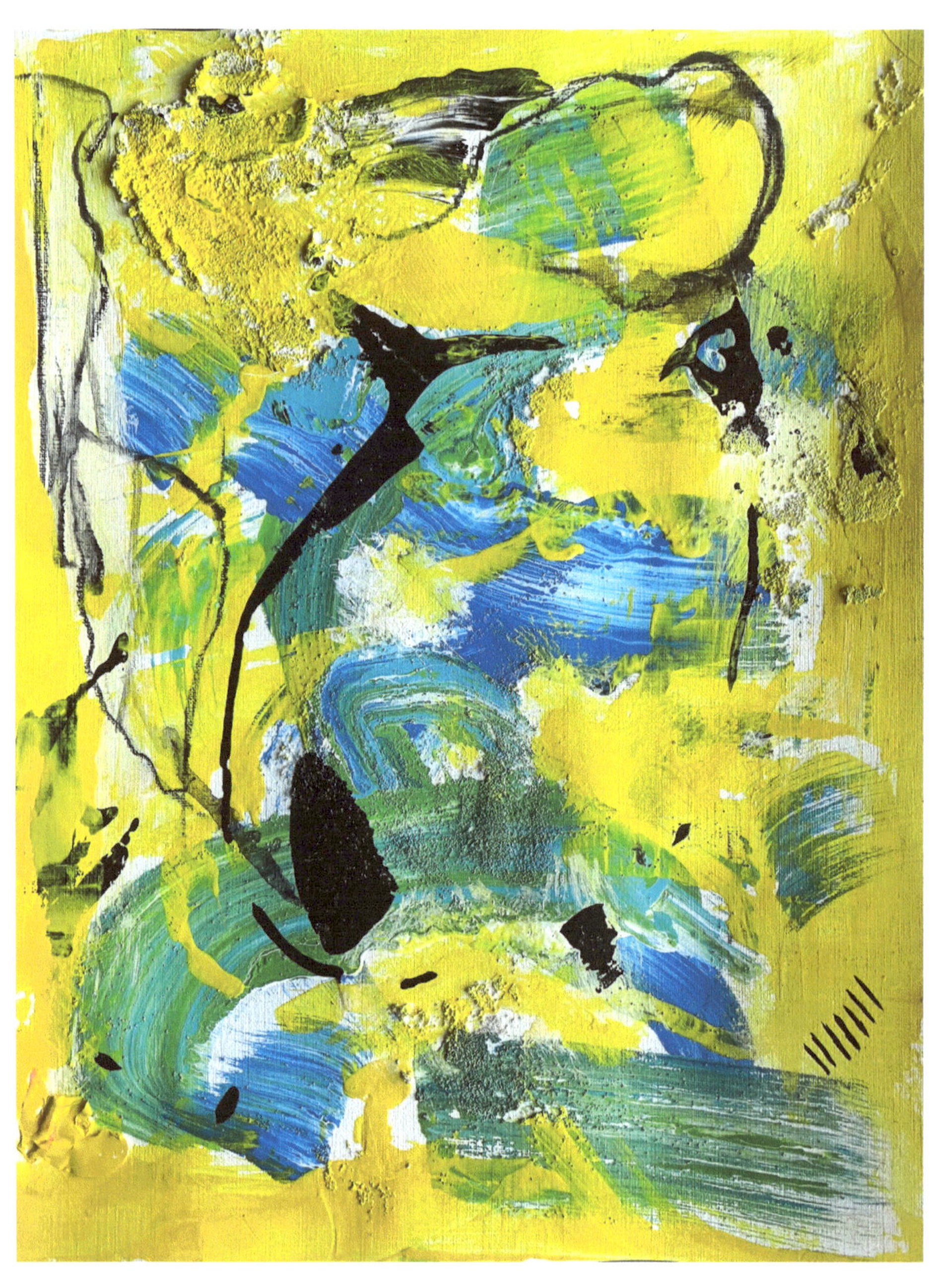

the hive

anxiety
s w a r m s
like a hive
not a pack
an army
of hundreds
too small
to detect
and
when
they sting
they sting
as
one

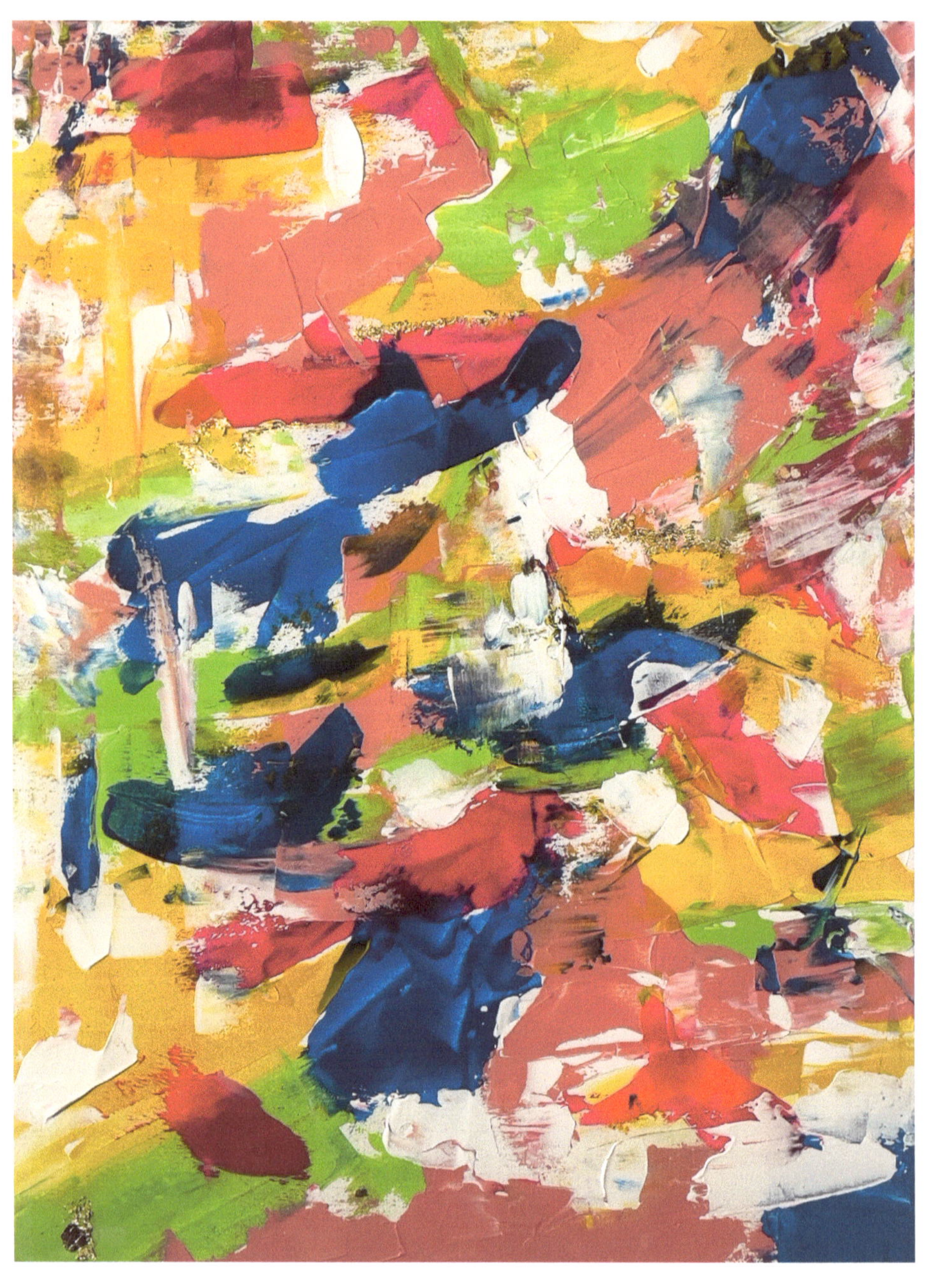

comfortable

while deep inside
I told you
I felt comfortable
with you
looking down
you told me
you felt comfortable too
if I could wrap a moment
around eternity
that's the one I'd choose

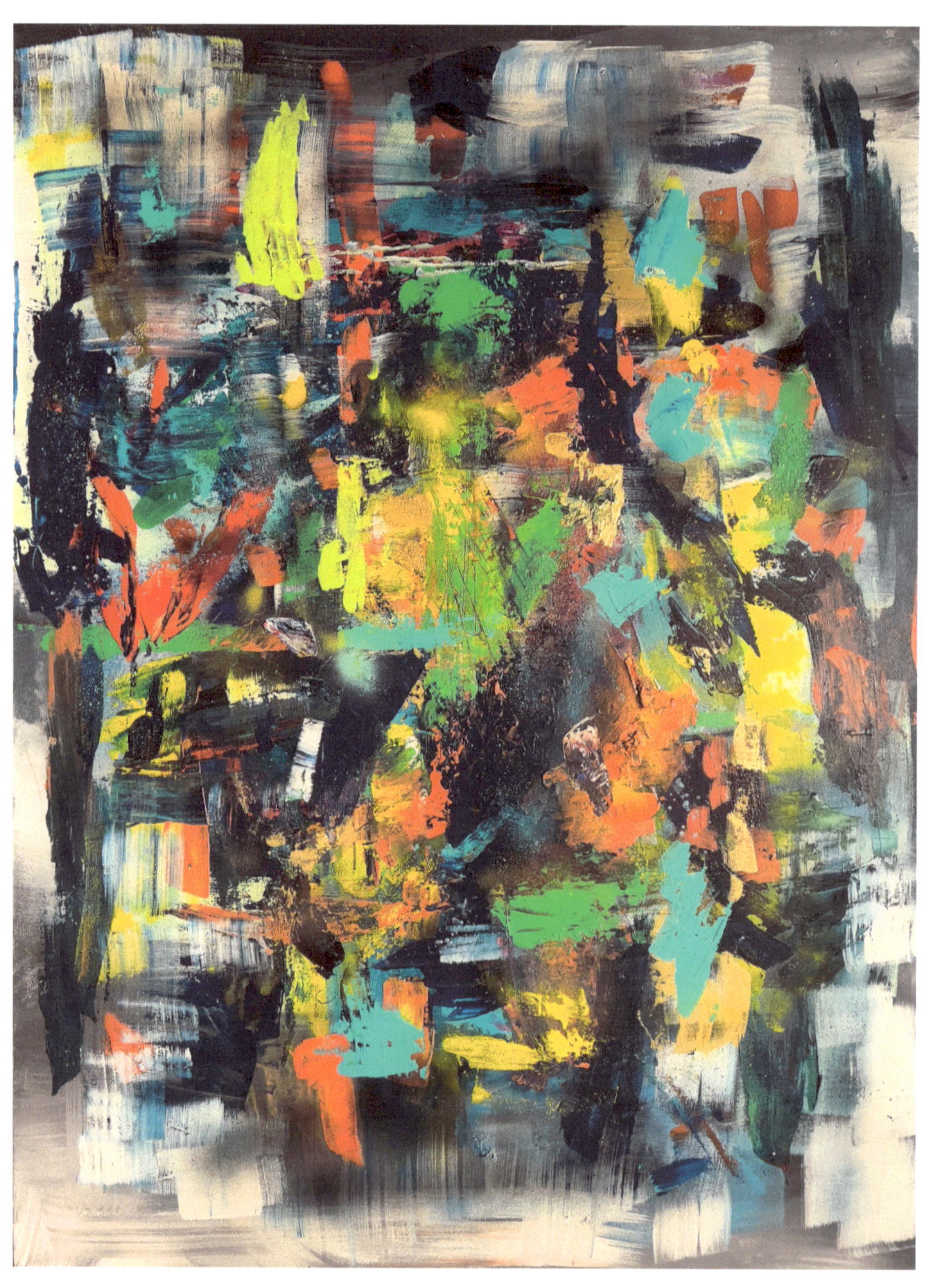

fallacies

do you ever dig so deep for the poem
that something else entirely gets out
a hurt that doesn’t stay confined to verse
and will lead you down an uncertain route
to a location taken from a backwards map
that was traced over all of the scars
love left you with when she decided
to replace each of your stars
not because they were dying
but because they grew beyond the galaxy
when you thought you were love's prophet
you were only spreading her fallacies

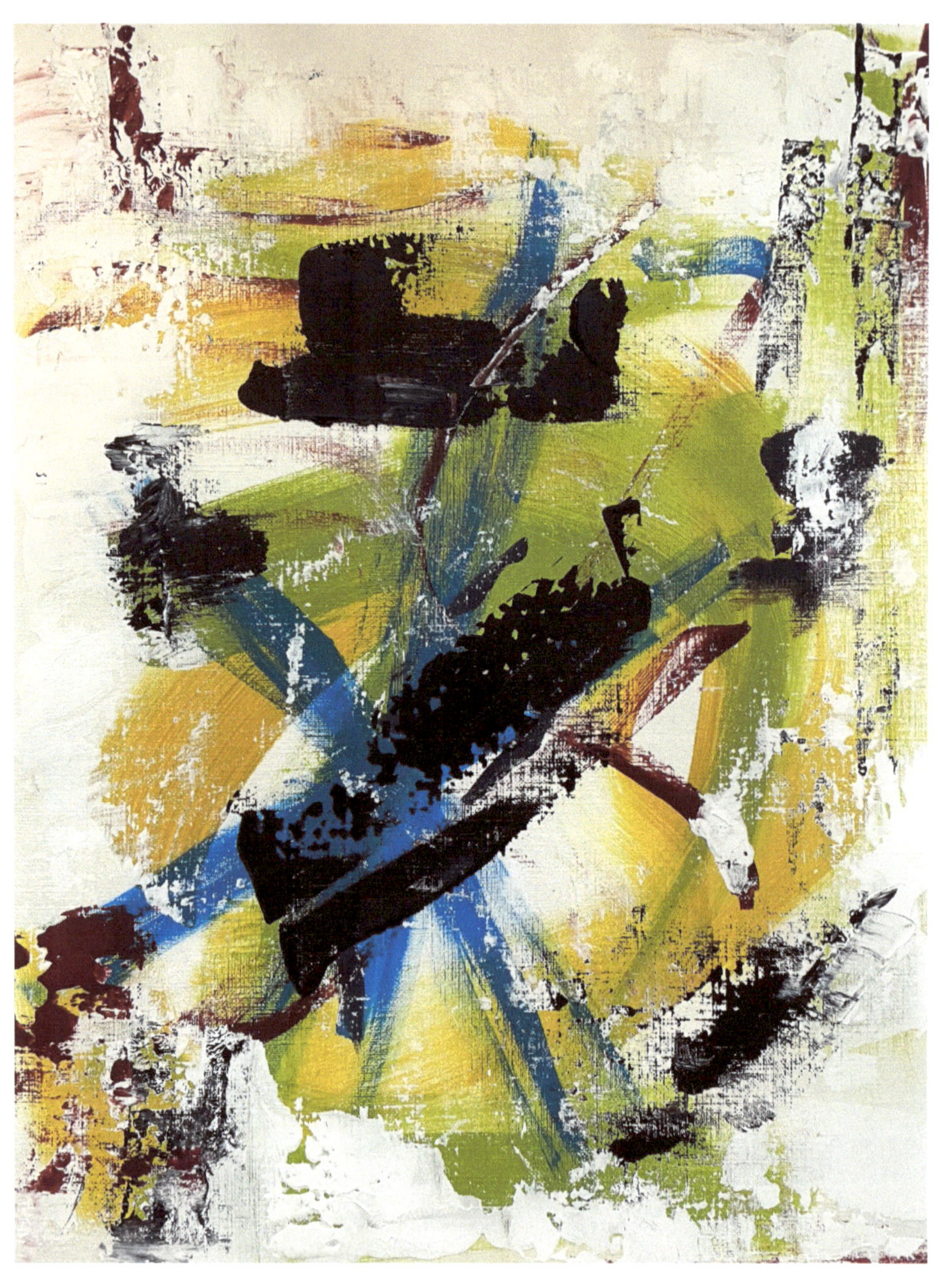

still

if I could pause everything
and stroll through the frames
no other people
obligations or names

I would still walk
with nervous energy
nearly stumbling
over my own feet

I would still worry
that I'm breathing too loudly
or tilting my head
like a canine in heat

I would still avoid eye contact
whenever possible
even if I am the only one
who can see

and I can guarantee
I'd still avoid any possible routes
where you could end up
in front of me

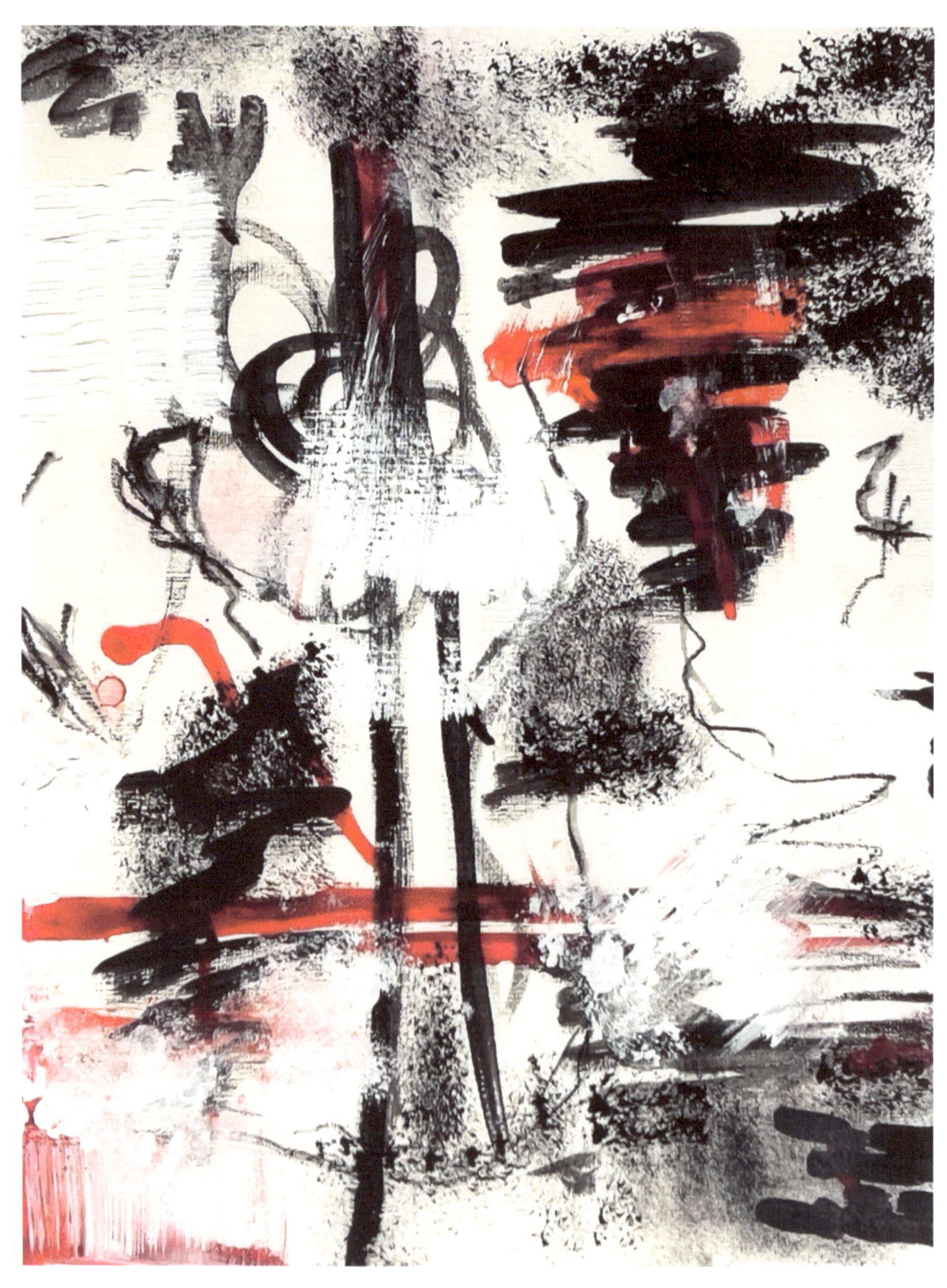

parted skies

the
skies
only
parted
so
god
could
get
a
better
shot

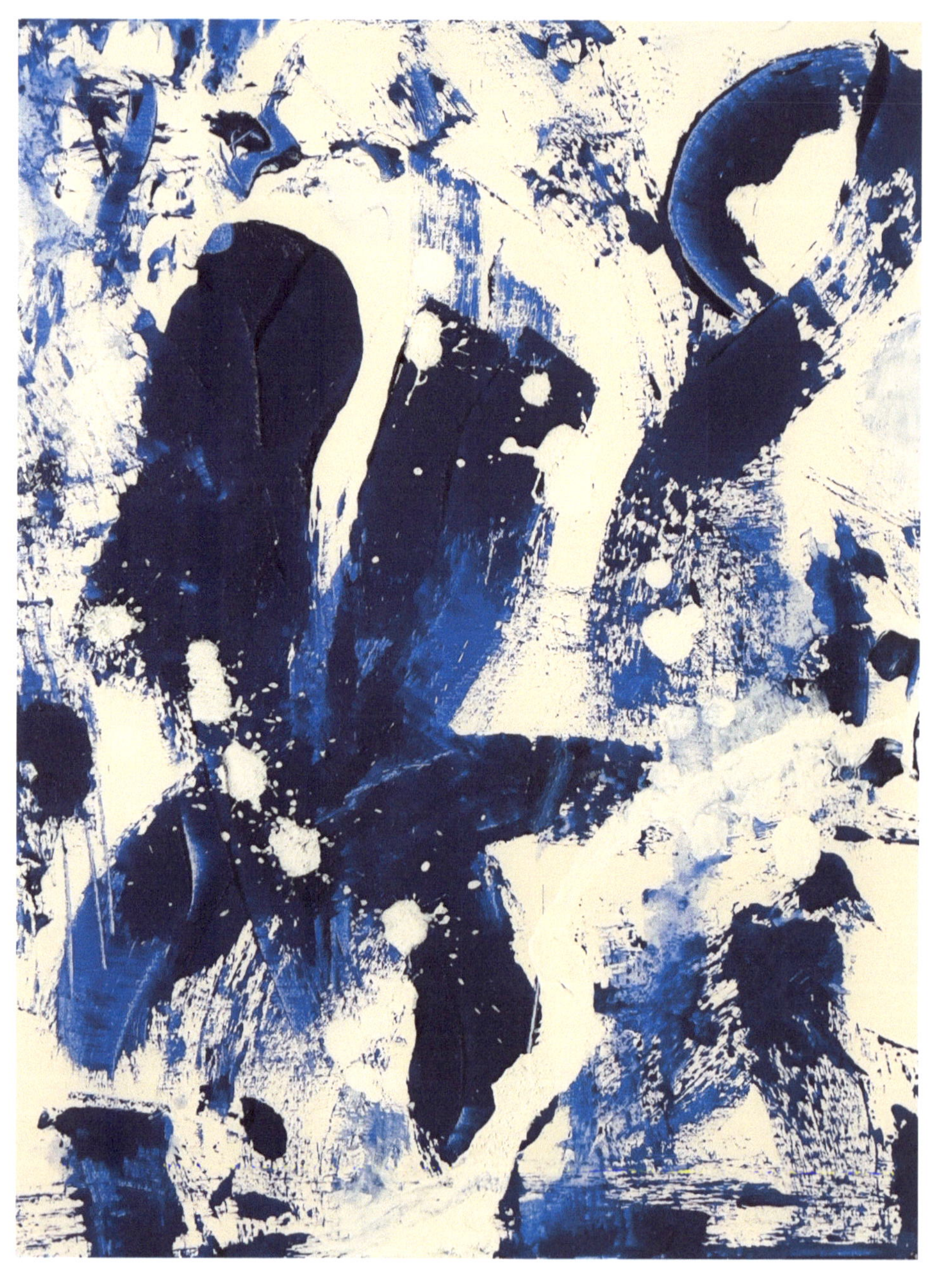

gone fishin'

I was sure that I was fishing
                    but I was wrong
then I thought I was the rod
                    but I was wrong
I really felt like the hook
                    but I was wrong
for I was only the worm
                    and now I'm gone

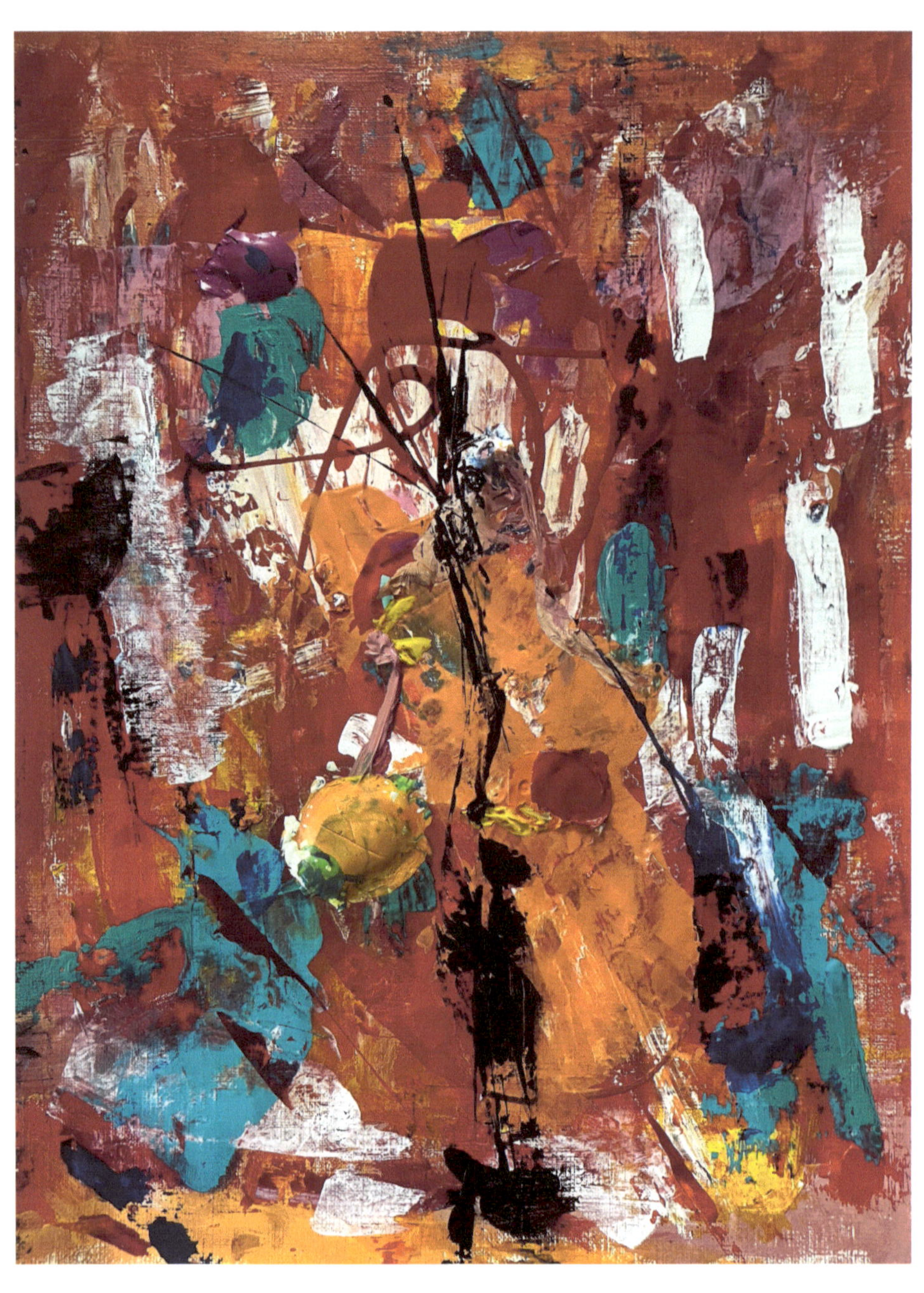

4/11/21 (ABOLISH)

it's	when	turn	looking	and
another	the	a	past	only
amber	imperialist	terrified	beautiful	recognizing
afternoon	blue	yellow	black	red

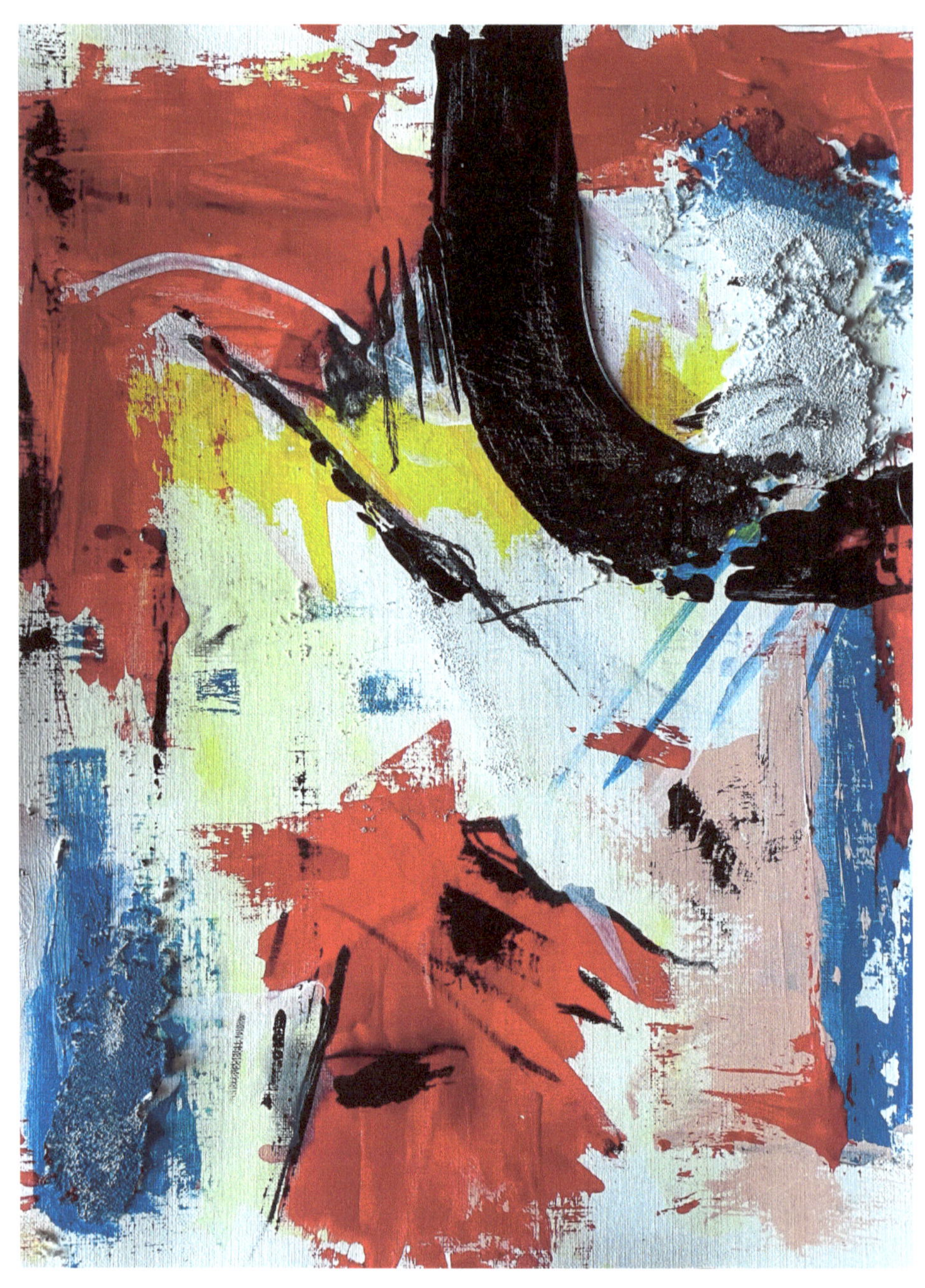

her shadow

the
sun

she's
so
beautiful
her shadow leans towards

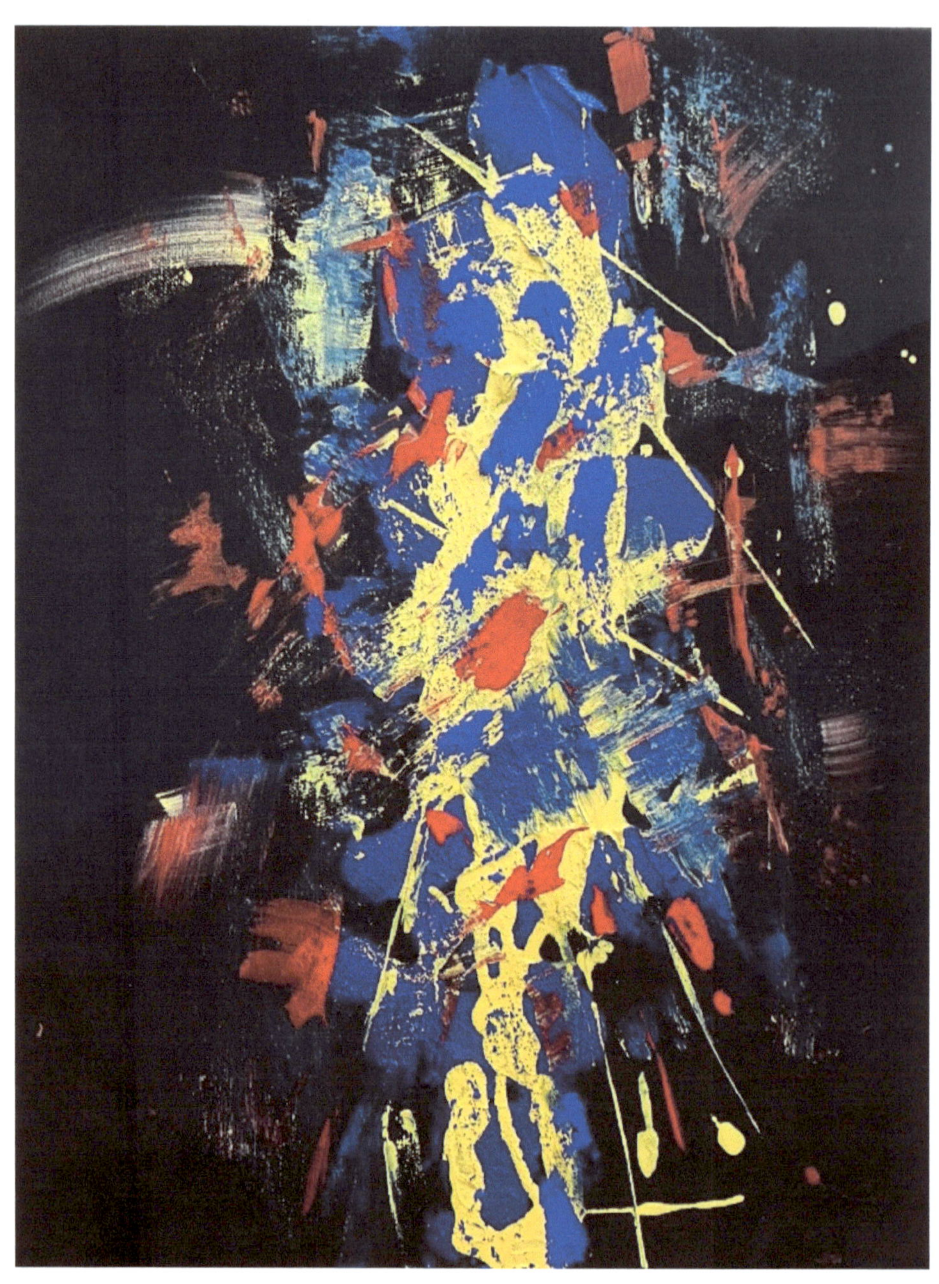

obsidian

anxiety
follows me
as though
I am leaving
a trail of blood
a stench
I become
temporarily smudged
and
it's not like fear
fear can be
compromised with
or pushed aside
this is more of
a physical force
like gravity
but it pulls
me backwards
just slightly
so that I am
the only one
who notices it
and
I am conquered
by self
a stranger
wherever I go
as though
I have been
unearthed
I become the core
I become obsidian

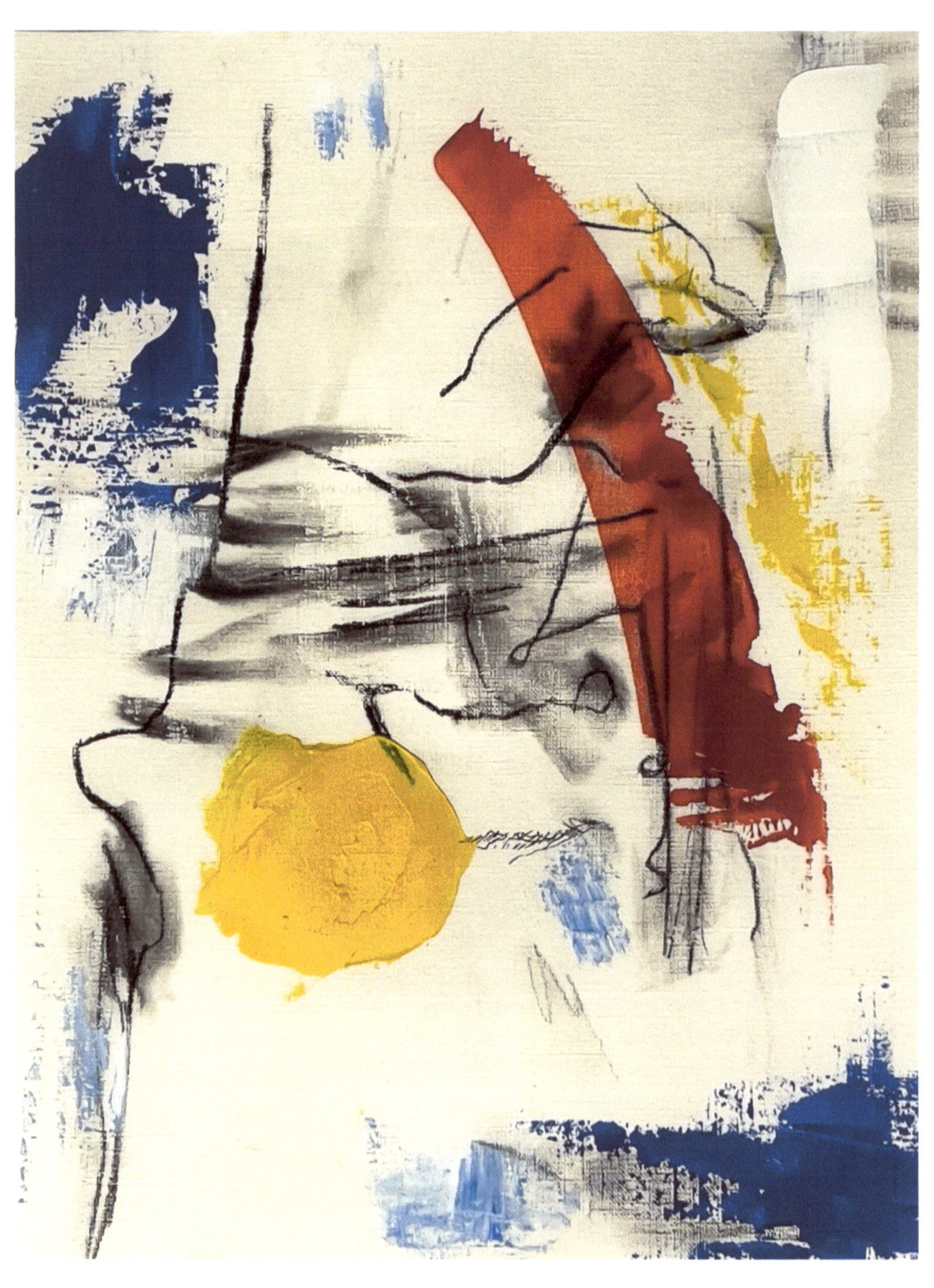

a poem to death

I wrote a poem to death
that she mistook for courtship
and though I often dance with her
I wouldn't want to go on that honeymoon trip

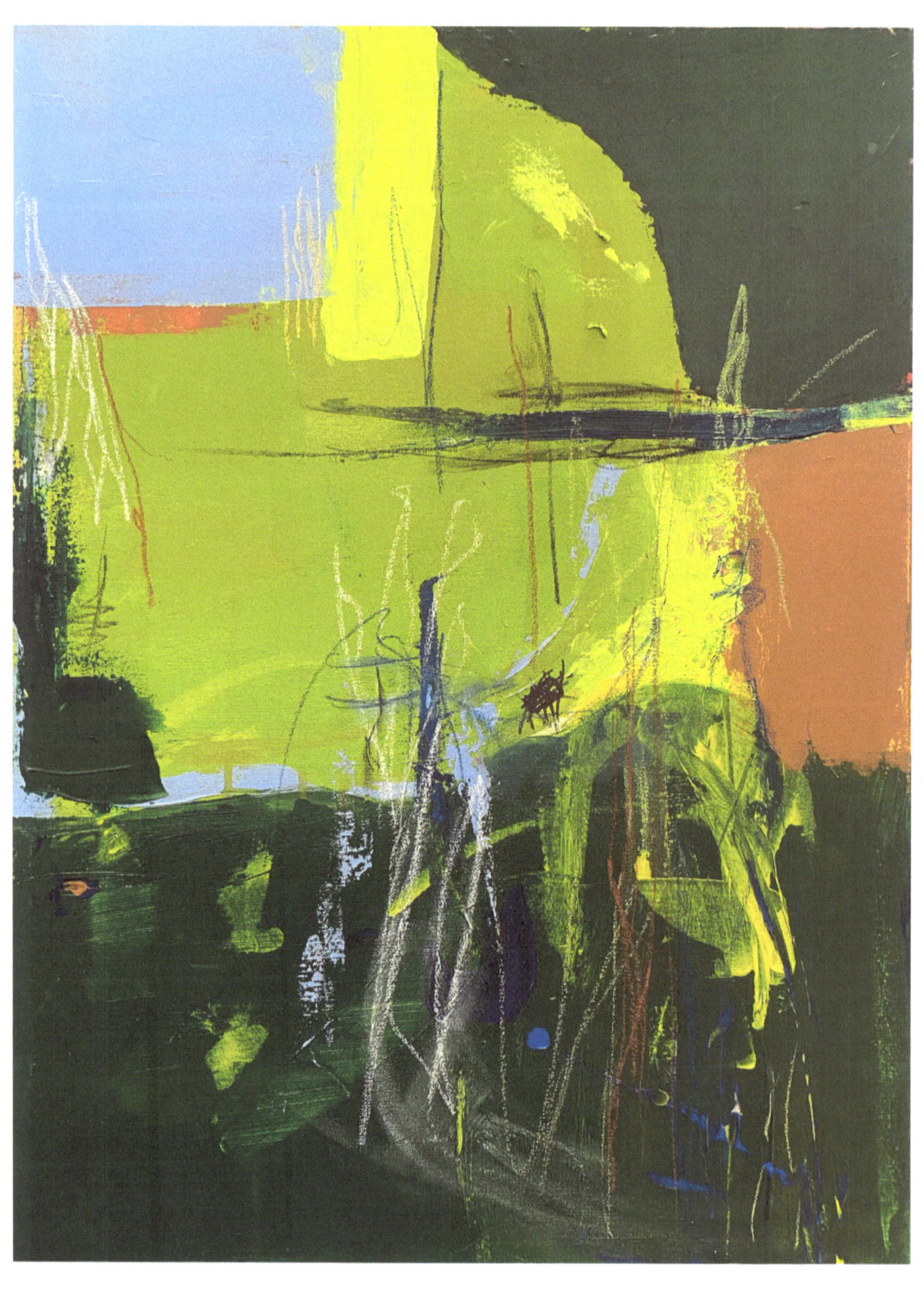

something resembling personality

capitalism ripped me from the roots like a weed

democracy watered my hopes and washed away the seed

religion held me under until I could no longer breathe

love taught me to immolate what should be set free

yet somewhere beyond the cacophony of me

I found something resembling personality

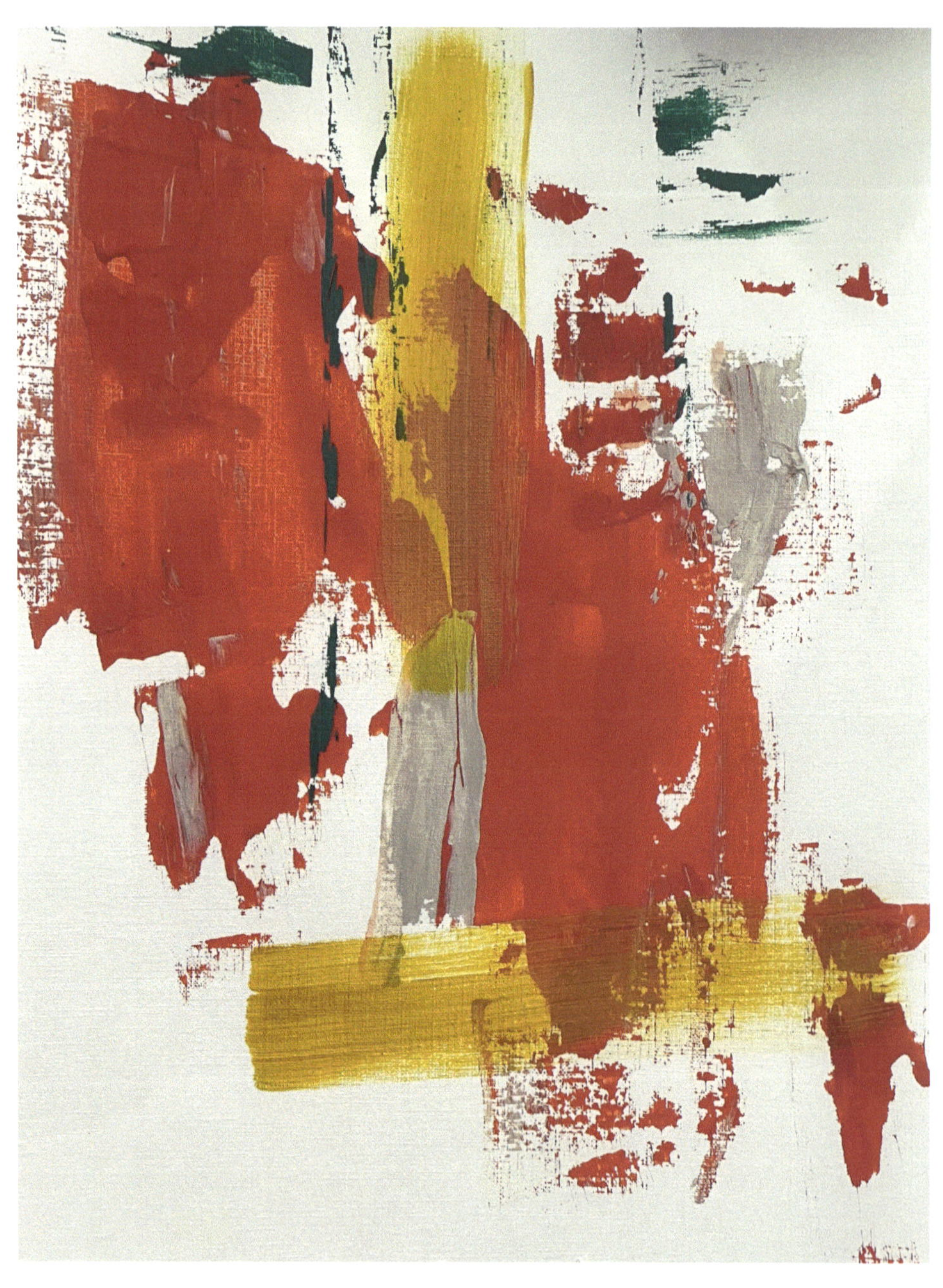

an excuse

I
set
my
heart
on
fire
because
I
needed
an
excuse
to
stomp
on
it

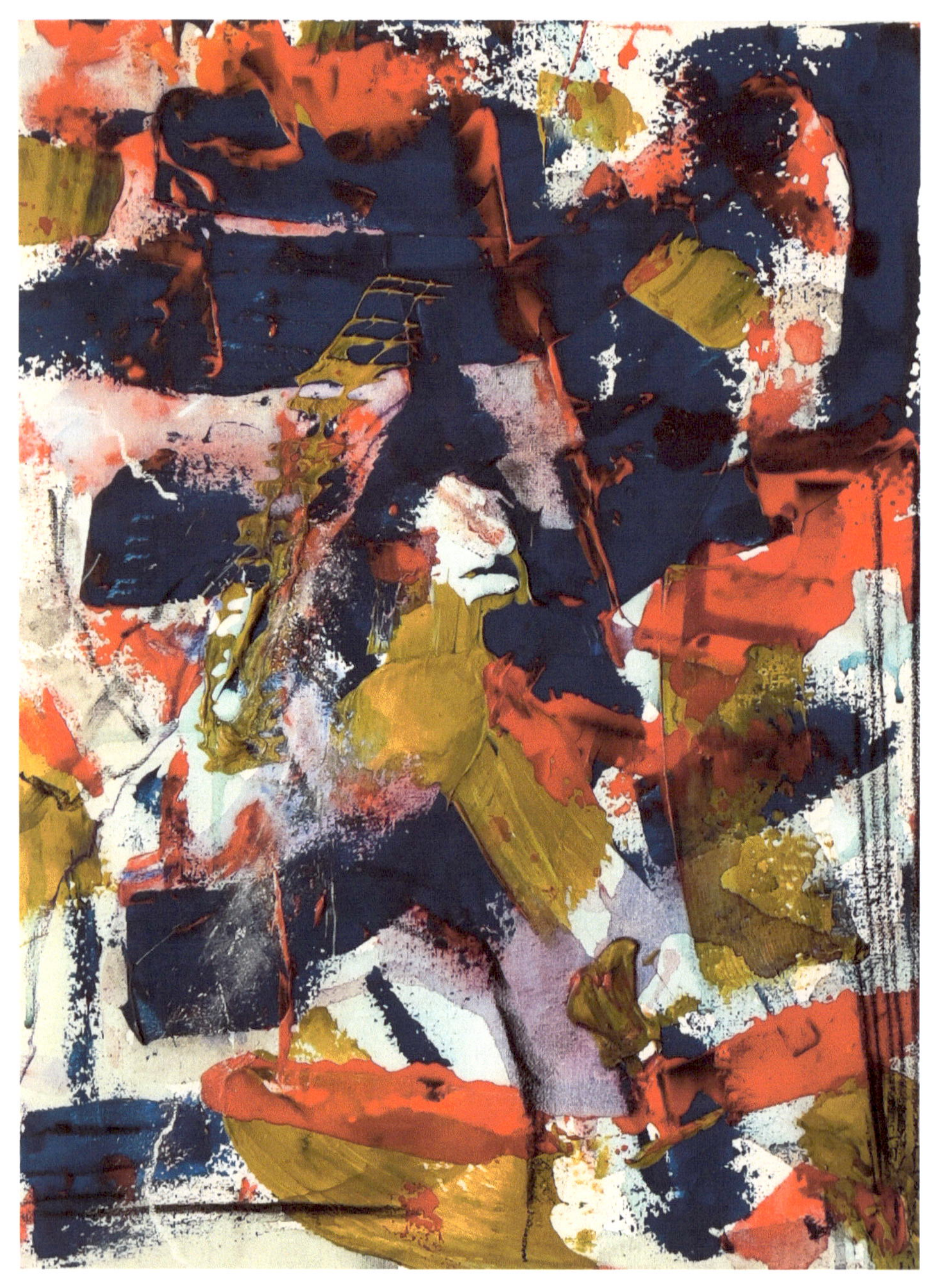

kaboom

I am the flame that
mistook
a
fuse
for
a
wick
expecting a lavender scent
from a dynamite stick

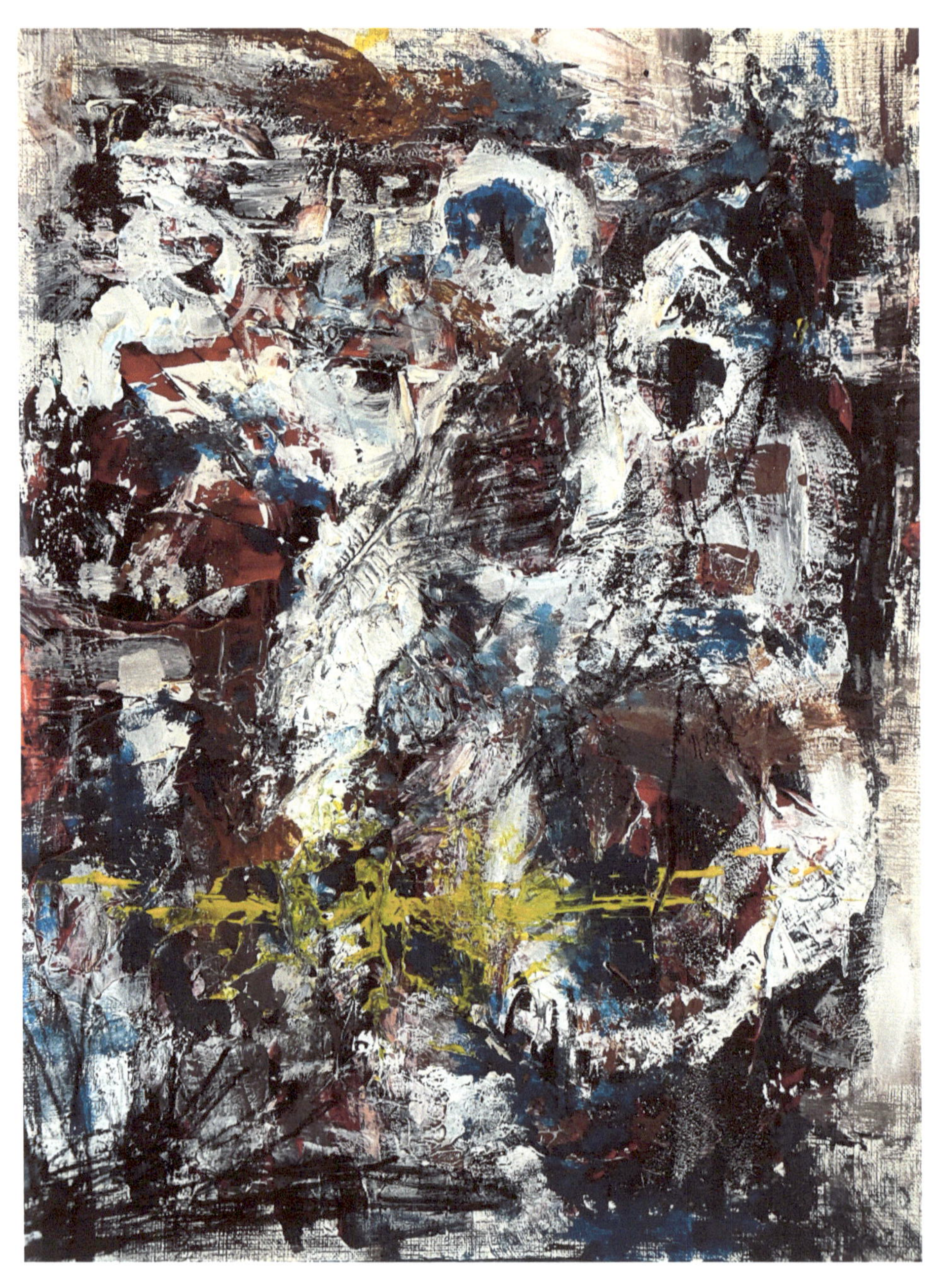

a hole that I couldn't fill

I found a hole that I couldn't fill
and there was no way around it

so I reached for god and tossed him in
god just got small
and the hole still wasn't filled

so I withdrew my money and tossed it in
I could smell my money burn
and the hole still wasn't filled

so I pulled out my love and tossed it in
my love made a single solitary thud
and the hole still wasn't filled

so I lowered my hope in a bucket
it came back up dangling and blue
and the hole still wasn't filled

for a moment I leaned over the hole
I wasn't mourning the things I lost
I was thinking of joining them

but then I realized there was nothing
beyond the hole

and
I
just
turned
around

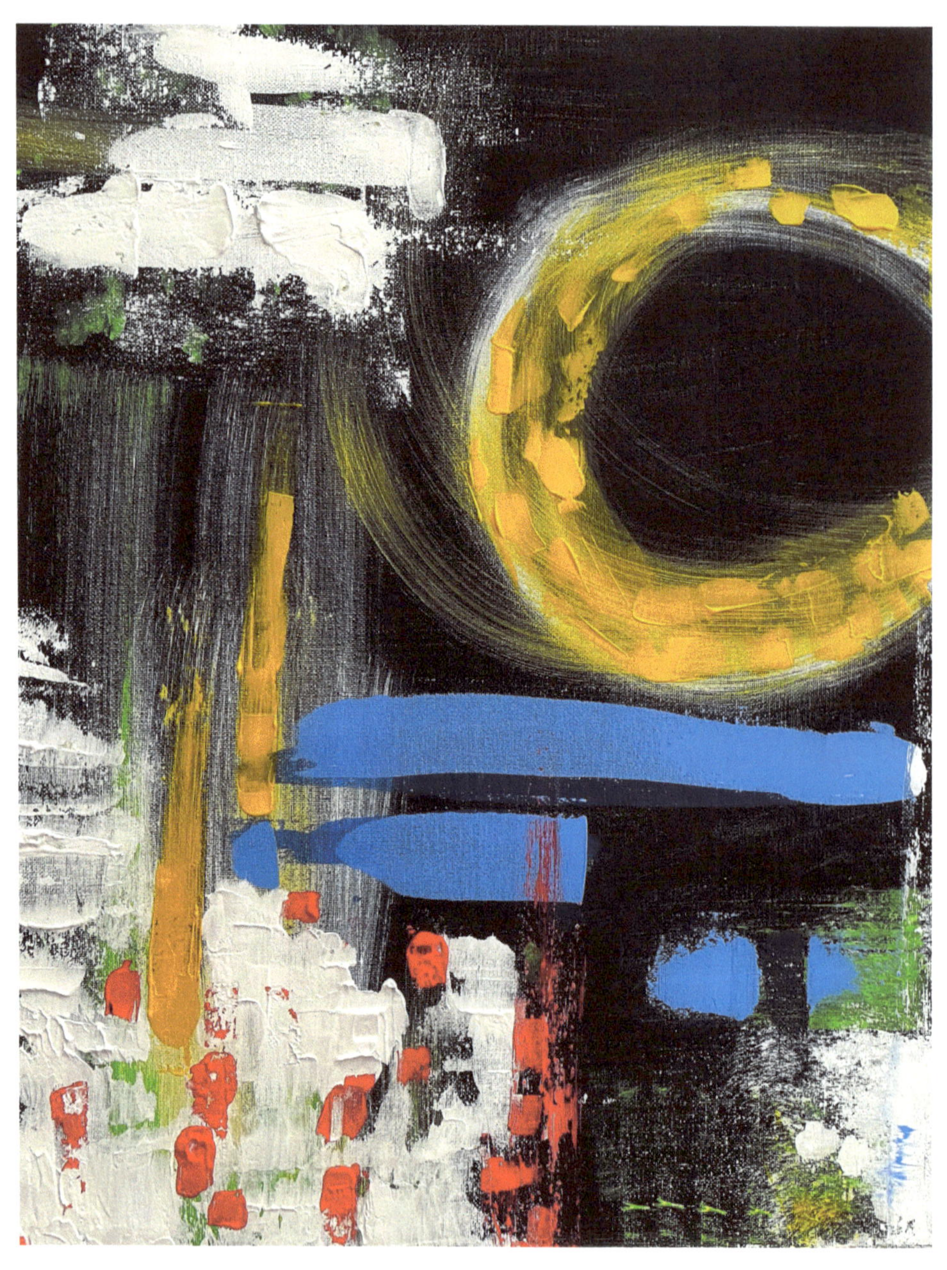

you may see poems

you may see poems
and while that description would fit
I see six hundred drafts of a suicide note
I'm too afraid to submit
so in lieu of final publishment
I've chosen these daily punishments
laid out on the page like doses
the children of my neuroses
but if this instrument in my hand
should transform into a weapon
let my verses run into the wild
and don't let me brandish the pen

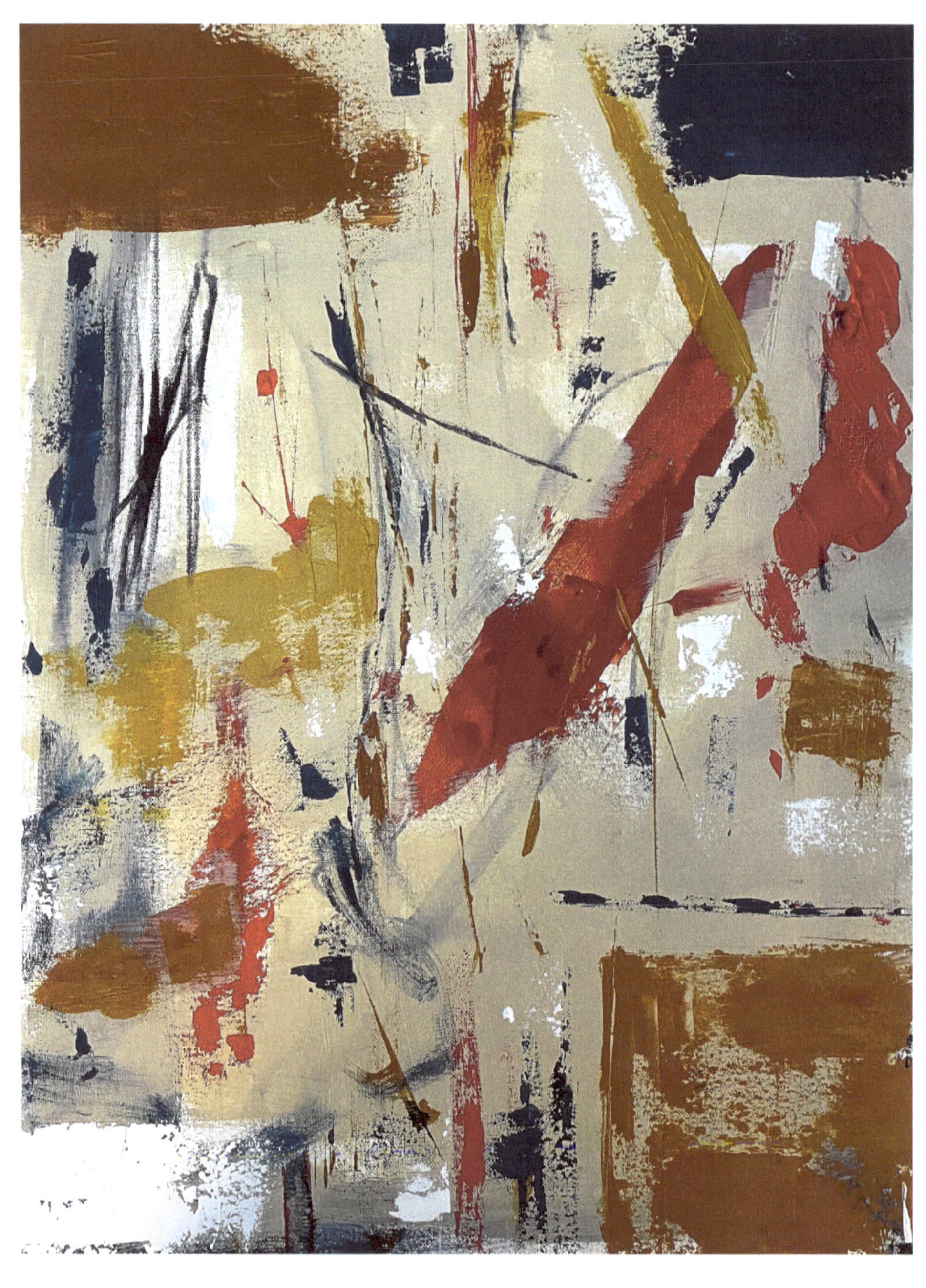

the nights and the days

the
nights
I'm at my most obnoxious
the
days
I'm feeling most unsure
the
nights
when thoughts are loudest
the
days
when pain endures
the
nights
I eat my feelings
the
days
feelings devour me raw
the
nights
defuse the situation
the
days
light the fuse and run

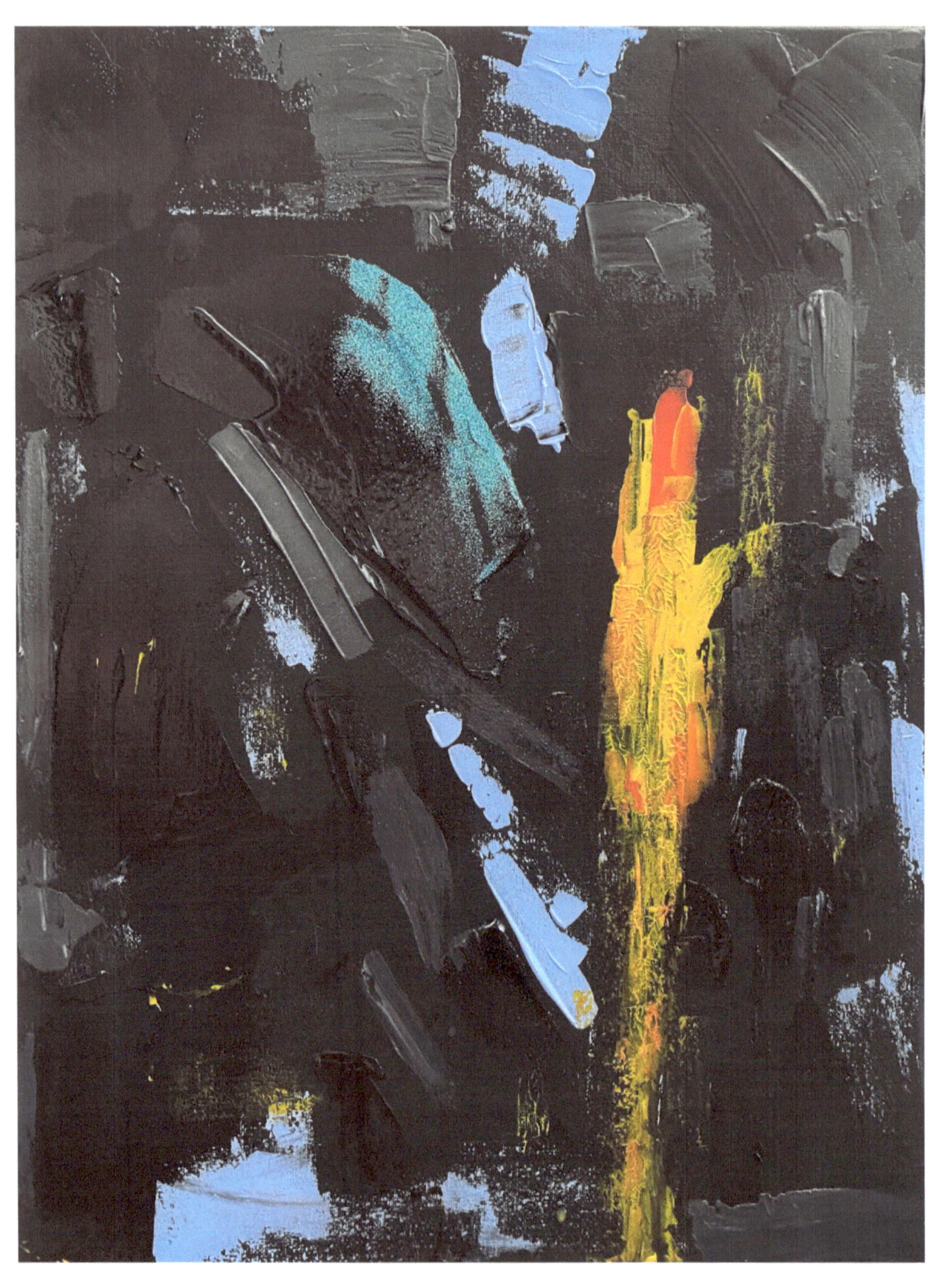

smoldered

he was once
a raging fire
with embers
that didn't need
a reason
to burn
but after
far too many
revisions
his book
lost its spine
and the pages
wouldn't turn
when he tried
to open it up
passages would
slip out
and dance
through the sky
if his flames
hadn't been
so smoldered
he could
have ignited
his pages
into fireflies

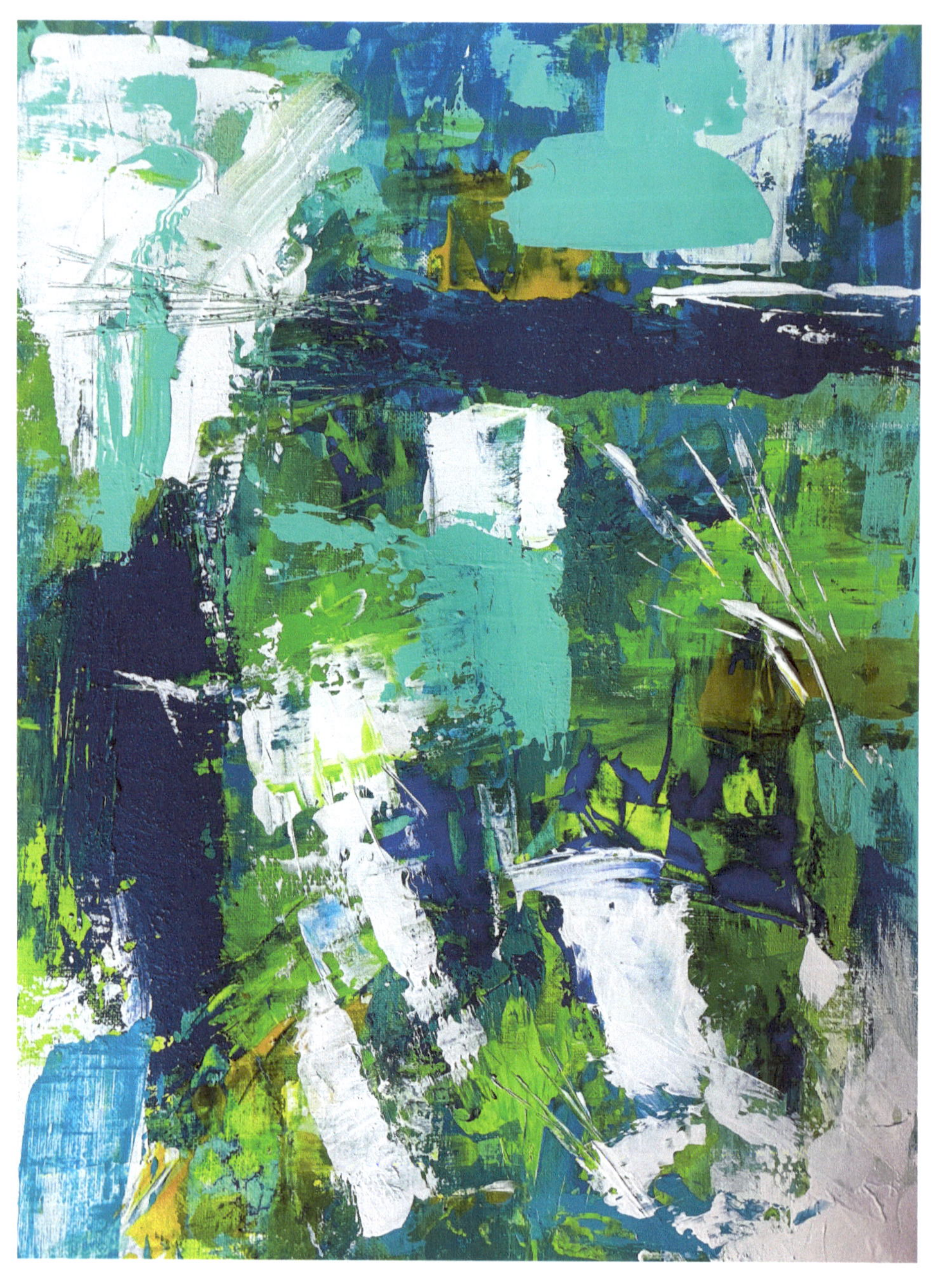

stillness and birdsong

if I woke up
beside you
I would notice
the birds
    drowned out
    by traffic
    both mental
    and municipal
    I rarely notice
    the birds
if I woke up
beside you
time wouldn't
notice us
and we wouldn't
notice time
    she may even
    forget to pass
    as we lay there
    enveloped in
    stillness and
    birdsong
            but tomorrow
            I will wake up
            alone
            I'll keep
            the blinds
            closed
            and
            I may even
            curse
            the birds

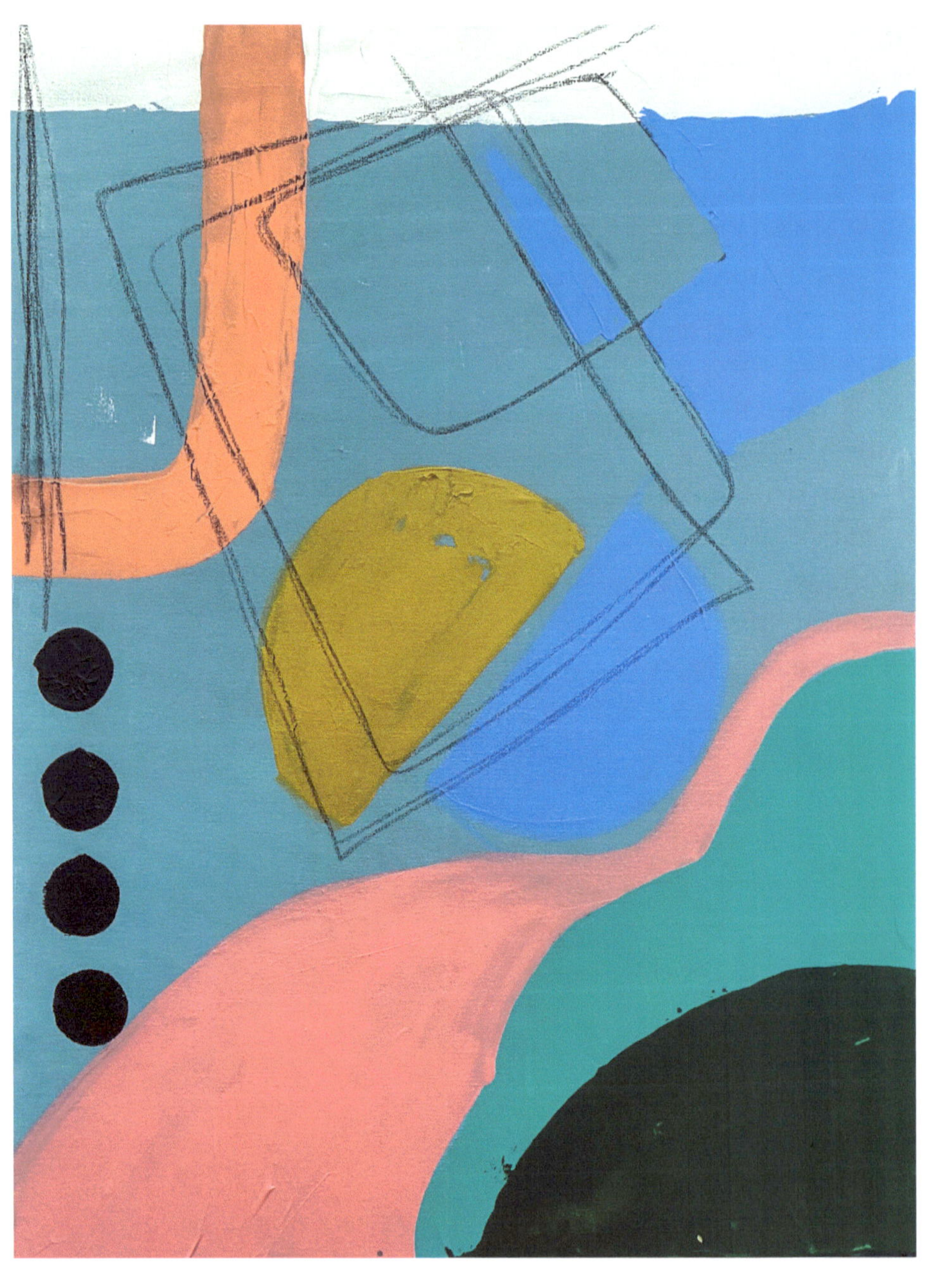

a self that already shines

when it seems I've absorbed all I can take
and as a result I've gone opaque
light no longer travels through me
or reflects off my face
know that I can still start a fire
bright enough for the choir
that rehearses beyond my bones
keeping my circuits from getting blown
and the light and sound
somehow peek around
the corners of my mind
pouring into the well where I hope to one day find
a self that already shines

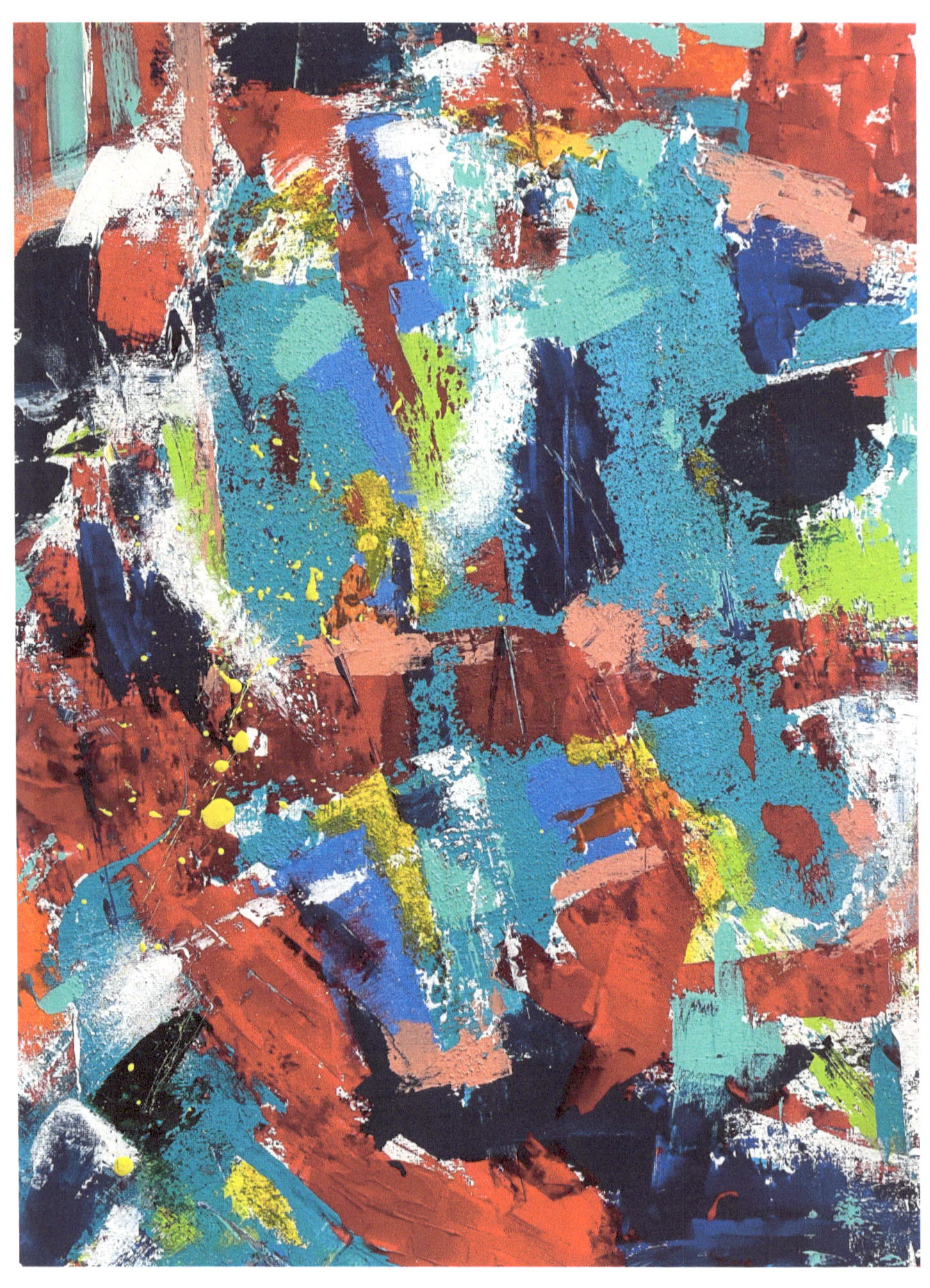

dancing with anxiety

when anxiety first puts
her arms around me
there's a strange sensation
as sweat gathers into beads

the dance we're doing now
is filled with unease
but I've yet to experience
the true strength of her squeeze

just when I think
I have her rhythms down
I close my eyes and sway along
but she throws me to the ground

before I regather my bearings
shaking like a nervous wreck
she helps me back to my feet
only to wrap her hands around my neck

then suddenly I'm here at work
after only spending seconds unraveling
the customers staring blankly at me
have no idea how far my mind was traveling

but I'm back now

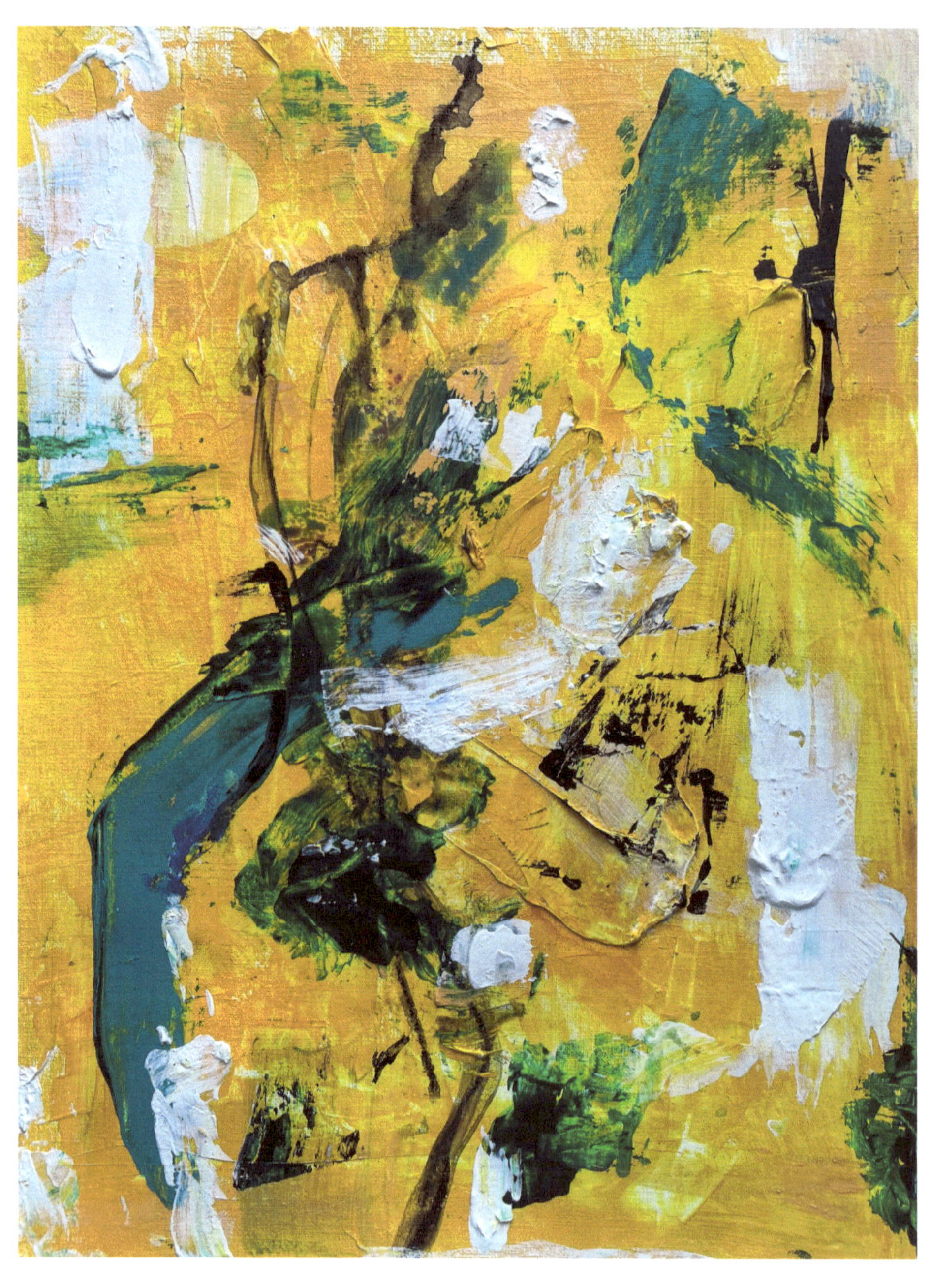

the lion and the sheep

right now I am a lion
but
in
the
morning
I'll
be
a
sheep
how
can
so
much
distance
on
the
food
chain
be separated
by only
six hours
of sleep

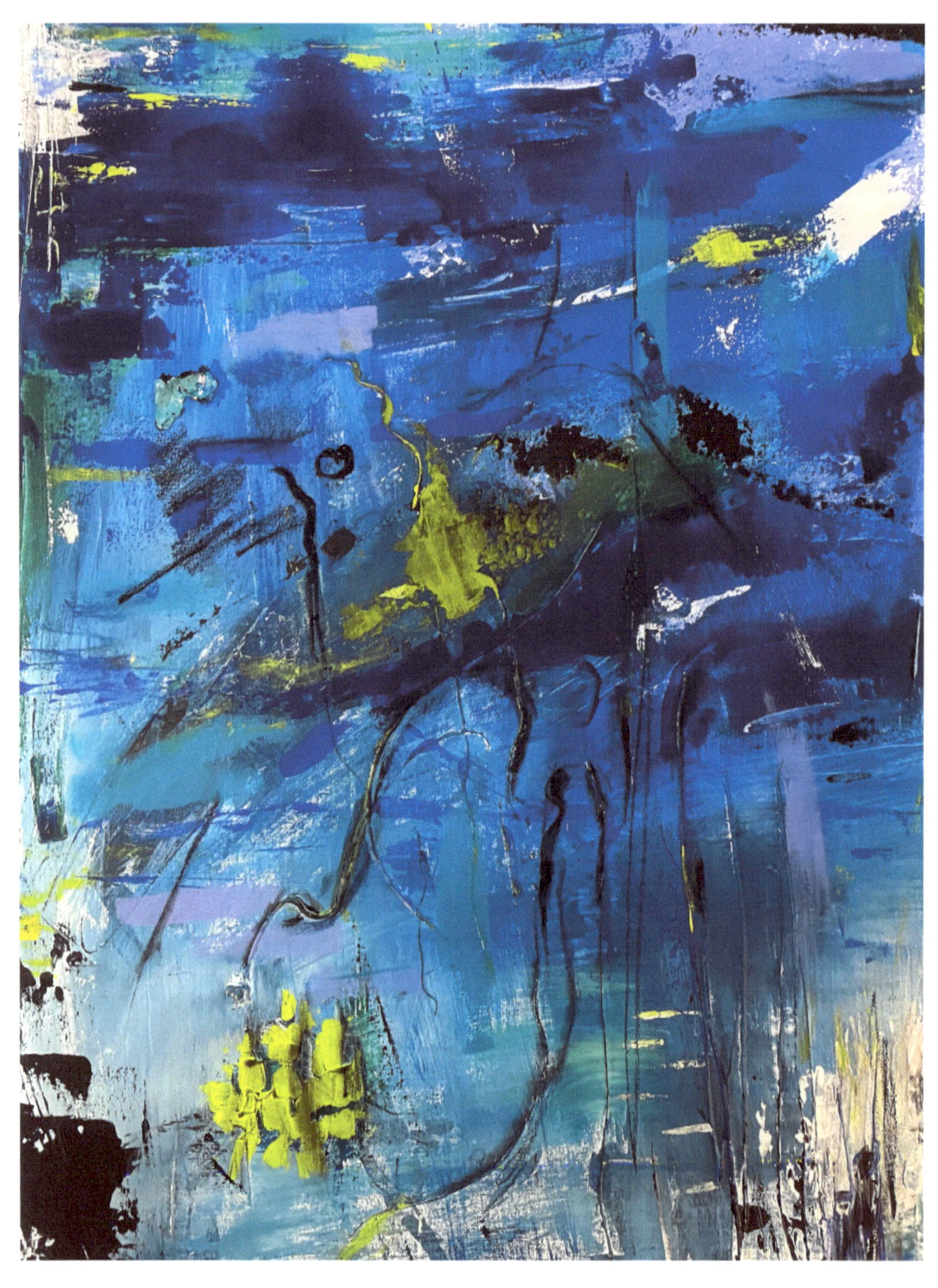

they always find me

while it may sometimes seem
the sea between me
and who I want to be
has temporarily   parted
it's mostly an illusion
caused by a contusion
to the kevlar shell
covering my self-doubt

inevitably my fear
that the coast
is not clear
will leave me
second guessing
the very ground
that I walk on
until doubt peeks out
rearing her spout
and covers me
with dissatisfaction

just once more
I look back to the shore
realizing too late
I've lost track
of the score
and the waves

they
always
find
me

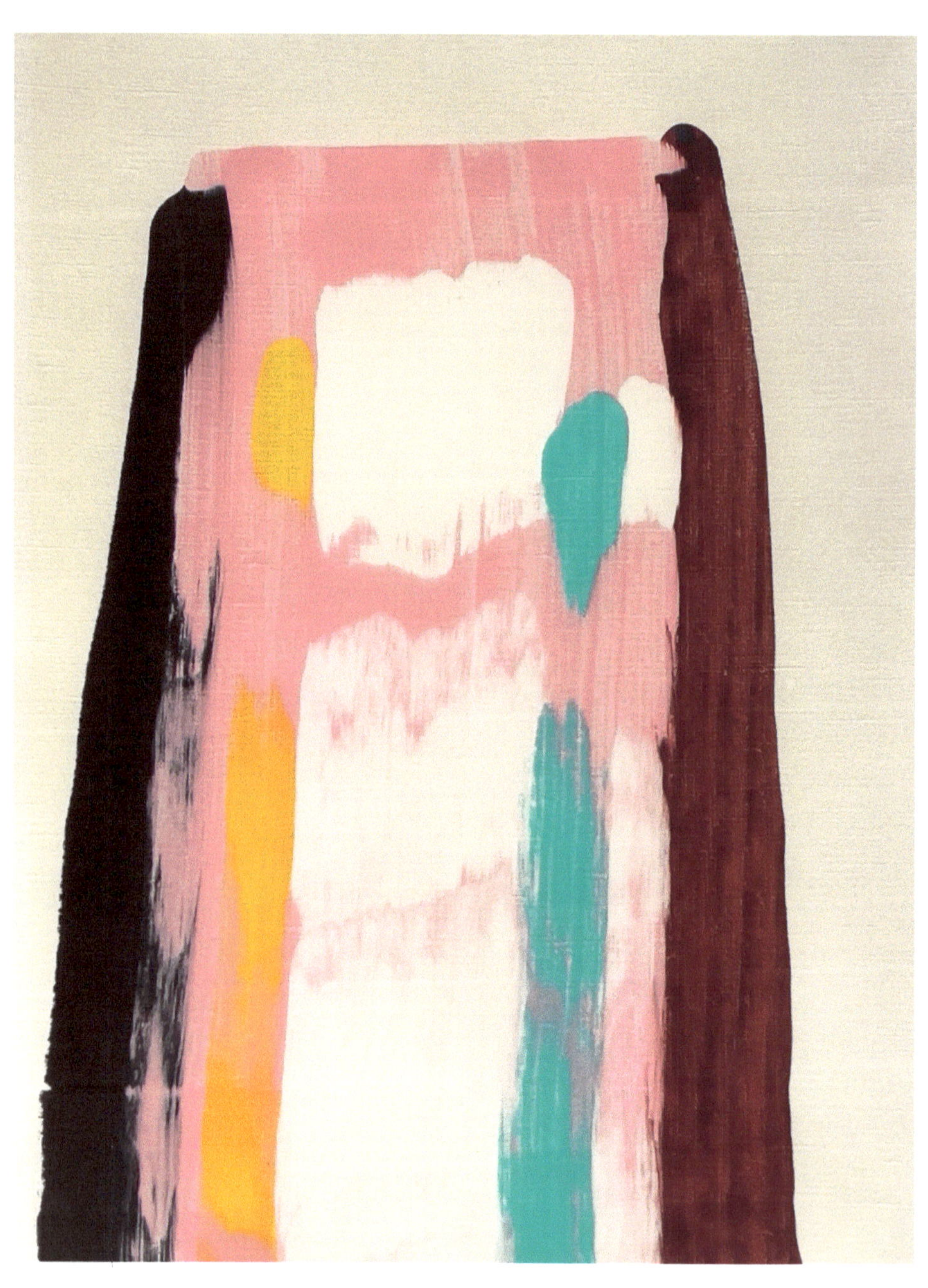

our art

let our art
                    be an affront
to those who
                    have made us
this
way

let our canvases drip
                                        with retribution
let our songs deliver
                                        final blows
and let our poems
                                        heal wounds
before
infections
turn
us
into
them

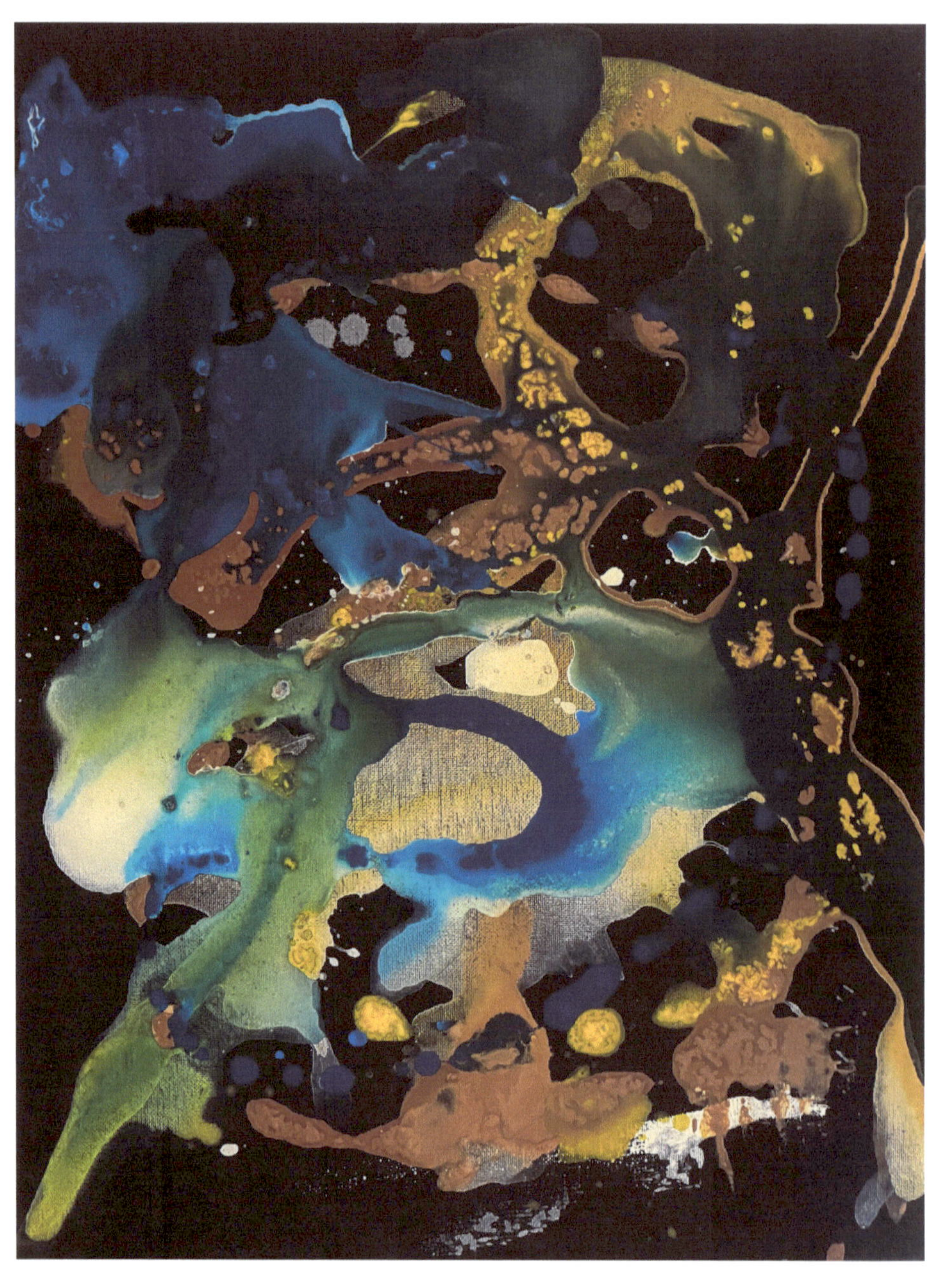

beyond the milky way

you were
a satellite

outside
of
orbit
intent to
end the pain
even if
it took
a part of you
away
and
the
black
hole
she welcomed you
to her table
with a meal
too sweet
for the possibility
of dessert

and so
she left you
stranded
motionless
and
weightless
beyond
the
milky way

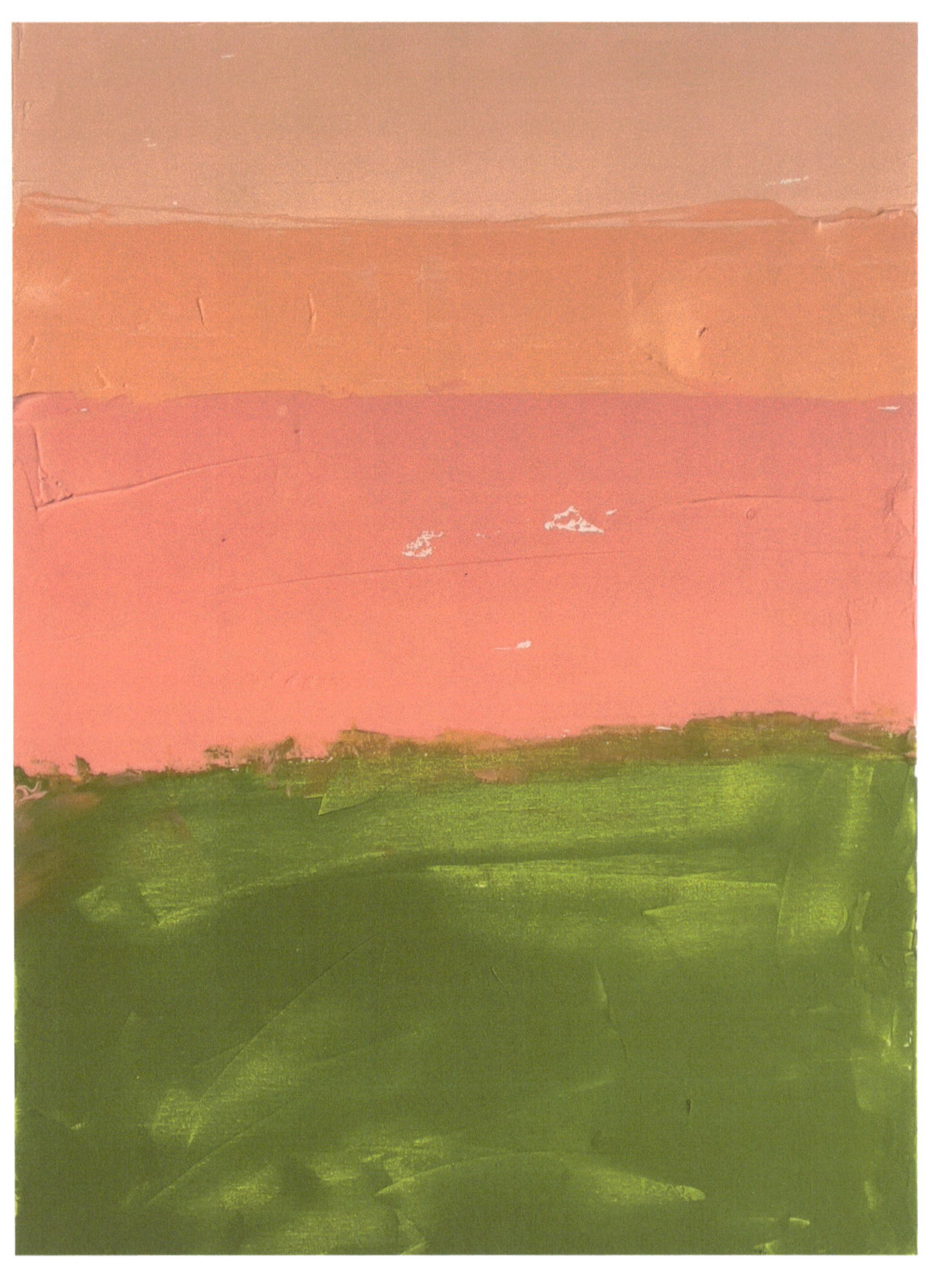

the constant swelling of the soul

you haven't noticed
the ubiquity
of dread
the constant swelling
of the soul

I can't help feeling
that it's coming
to a head
stumbling from
kleptocracy
to
technocracy
without tucking
our chins

if they weren't
so incompetent
we'd likely be dead
but instead
we're just
unsatisfied
underpaid
and pinned down
by the prospect
of tomorrow

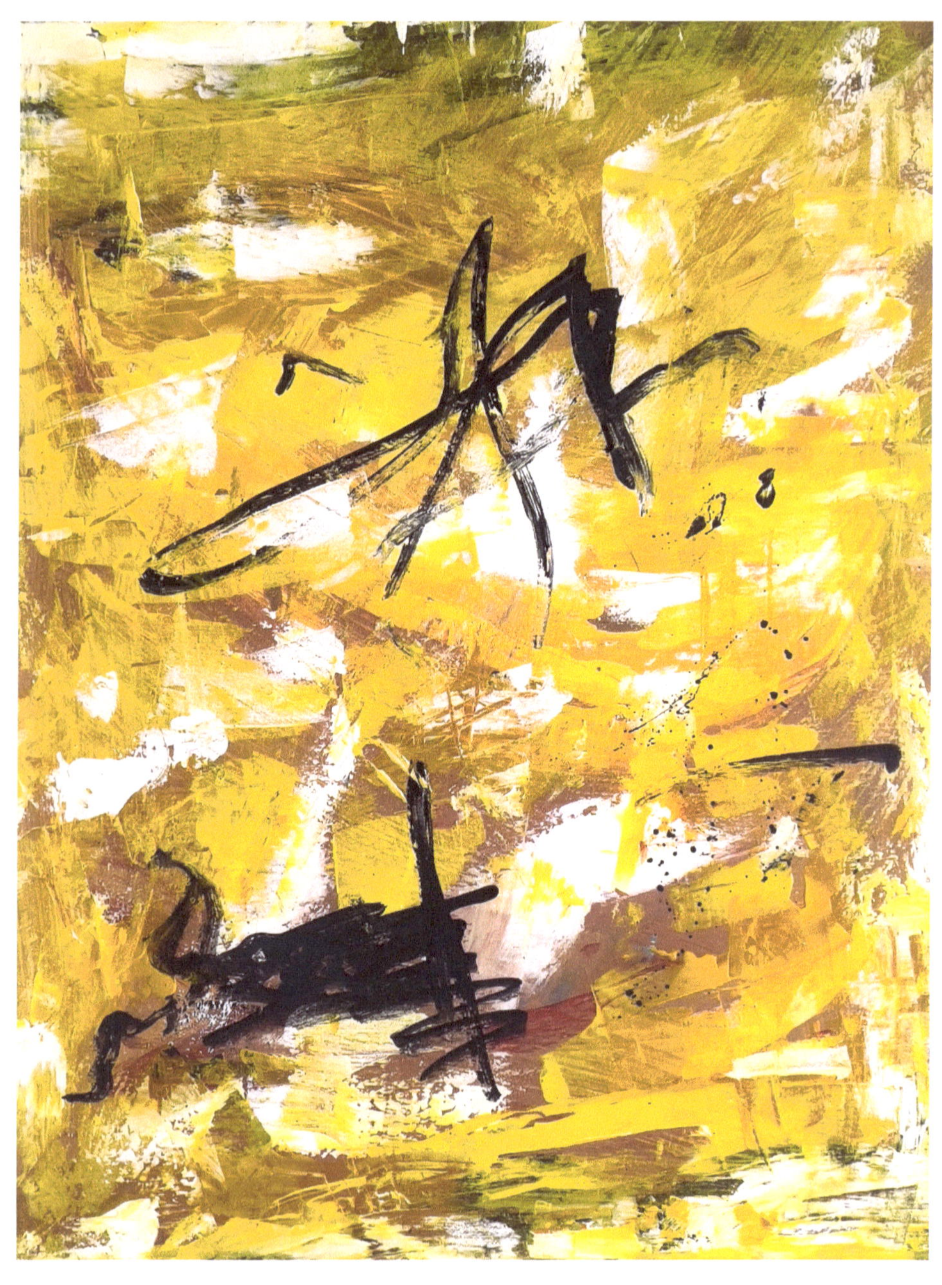

the fractured hourglass

living inside this
fractured
hour
glass
I
can't
stop
applying
pressure
to all these cracks

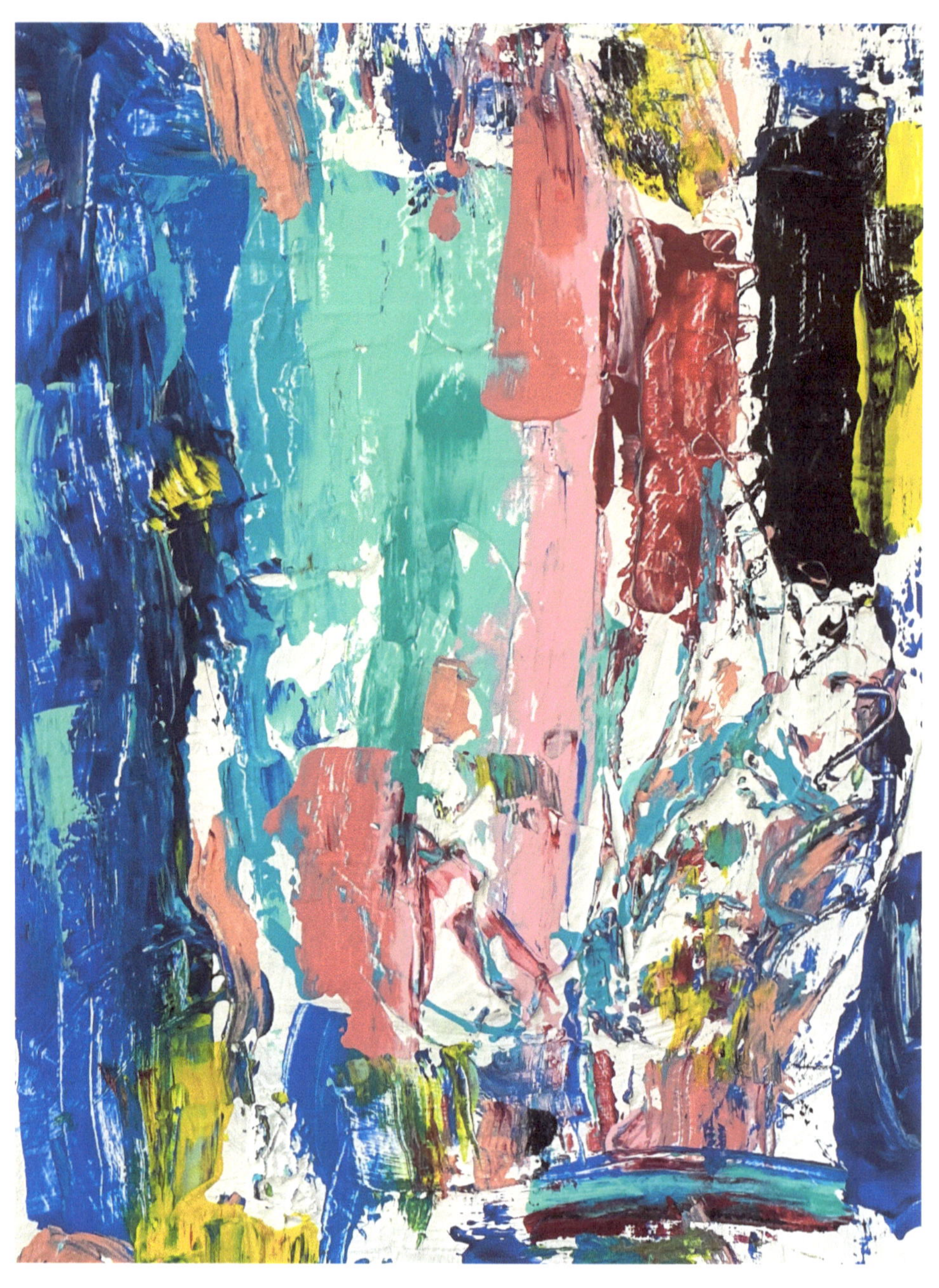

a note from the pharmacy

take one for nausea
    two for discomfort
    three to forget the rest of the day
    four to unravel the universal fabric
    five to stitch yourself into the seams
    six for debasement
    seven for displacement
    eight to flash flood your mental basement
    nine to prepare yourself for replacement
    and at ten you're calling cut on the scene

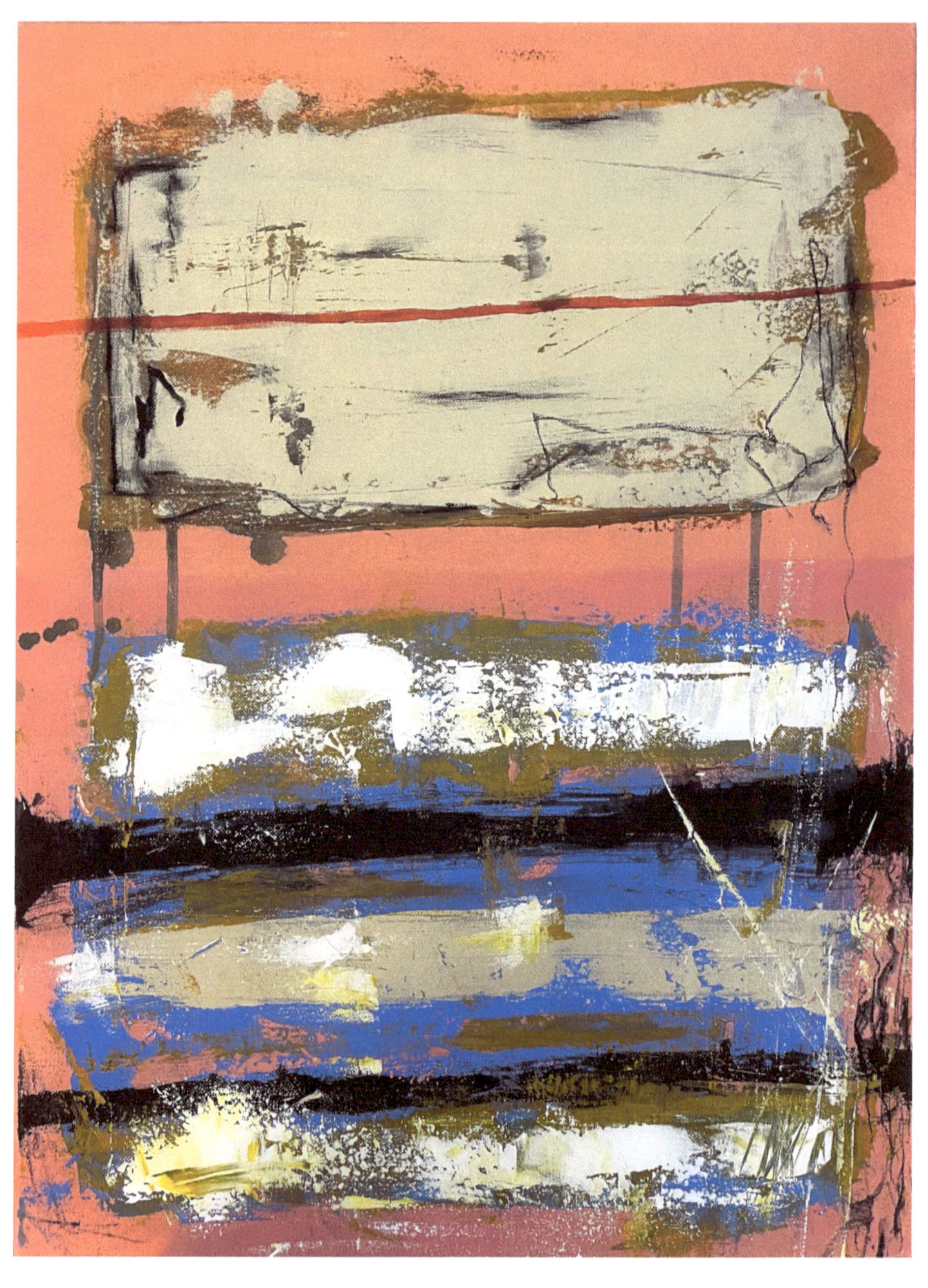

a hymnal for a departed war criminal

let's play a hymnal

for a departed war criminal

who knew what was at stake

when he baked his lies in yellow cake

though we could show no remorse

or as they call it "staying the course"

for he was just a button that empire pressed

when they needed their bloodthirst acquiesced

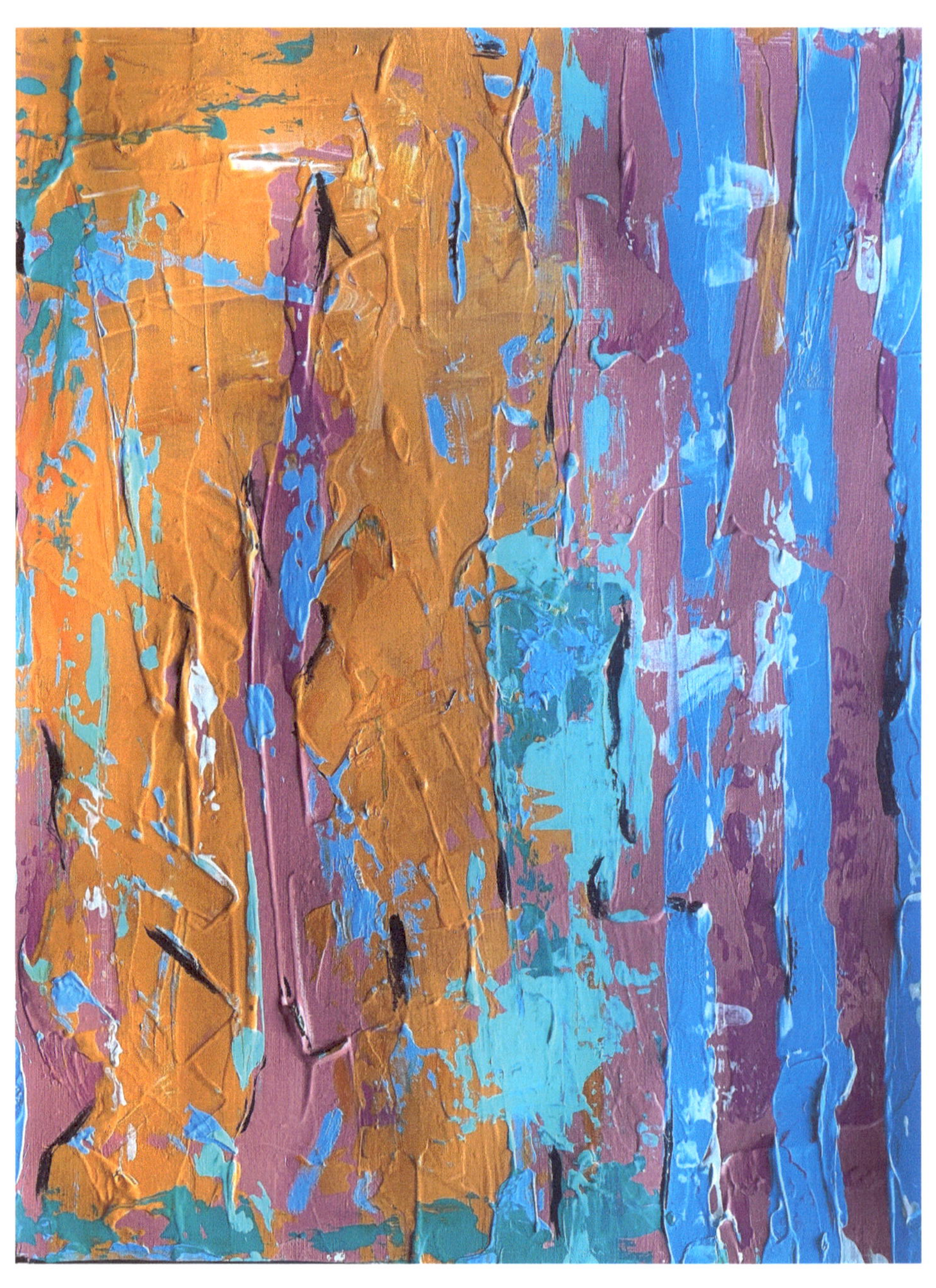

seasons

living
I off flower
could the sweet
spend nectar your
seasons of
but if we're only together for just a single evening
we'll
have
to
make
seasons
change
in
an
hour

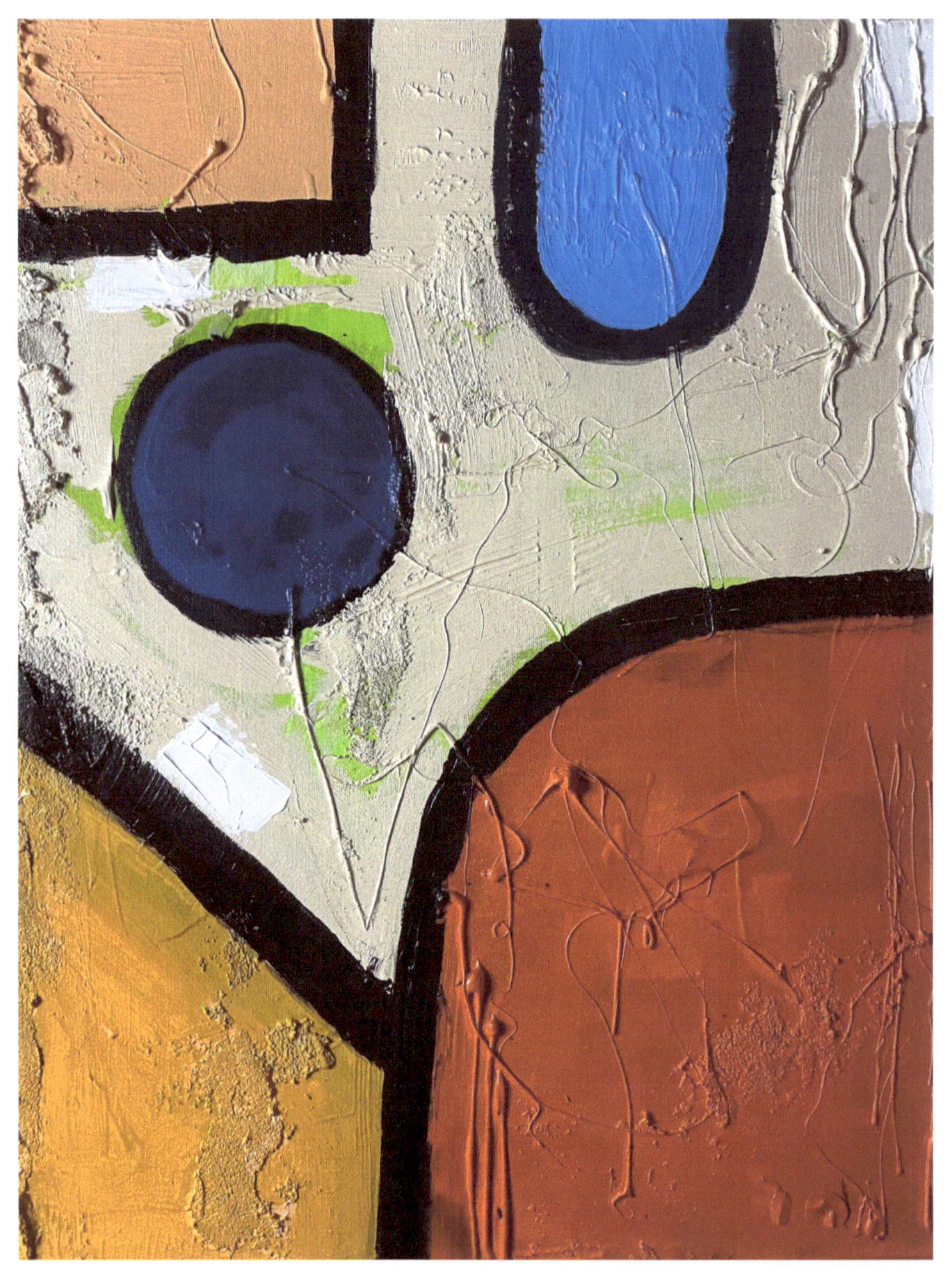

percussive

I lived
a life
so hollow
they mistook
me for
a drum
after covering
me up
with canvas
they beat me
until I
was numb
I did my best
to smile
between my
missing teeth
as they were
laying down
polyrhythms
on my face
while keeping
the perfect beat
but the finale was
quite unfortunate
my heart let out
its final groan
before I had
the chance
to hear them
play my ribcage
like a
xylophone

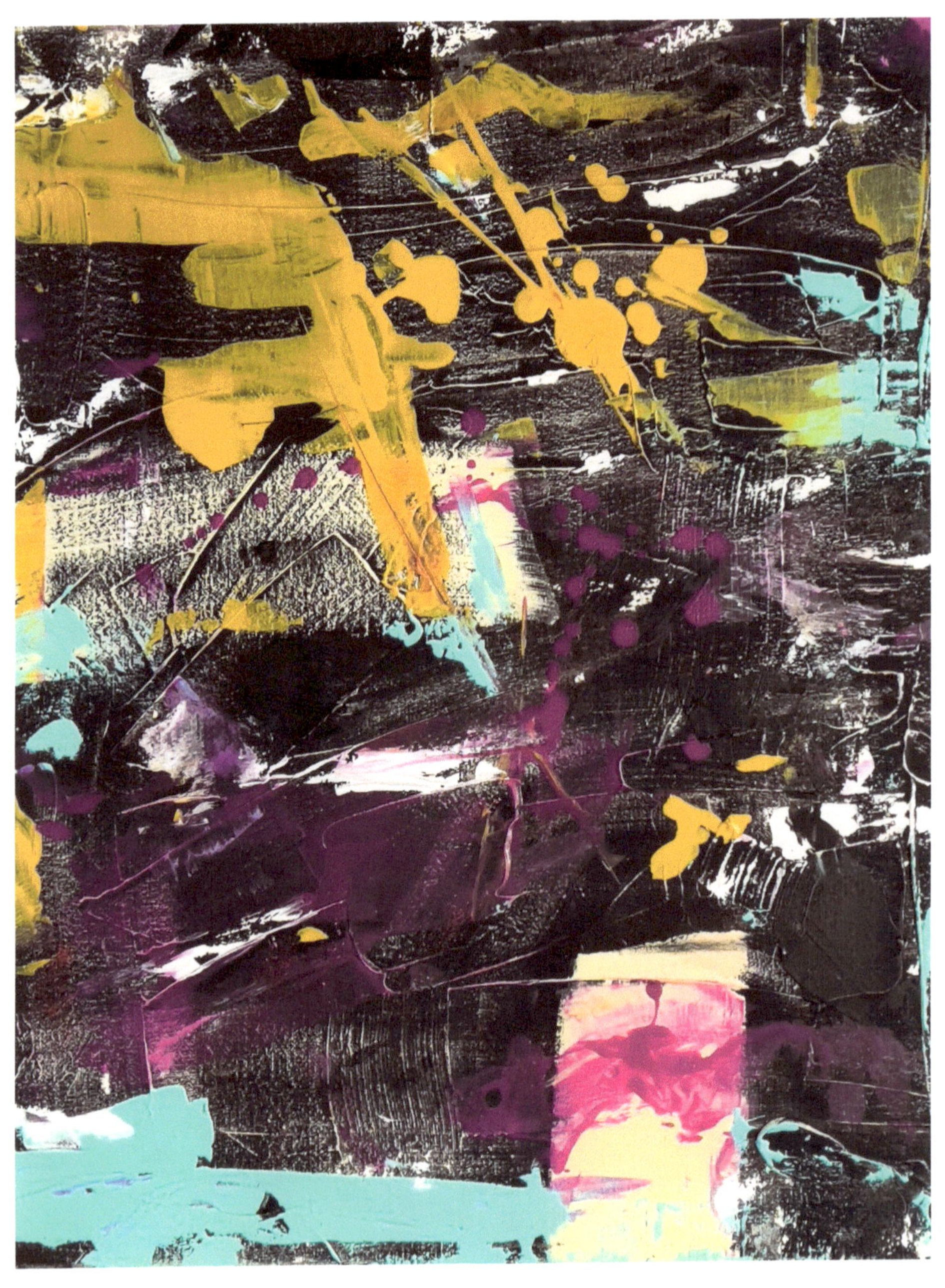

crushed

why does hope
always get crushed

they could
fillet it
flail it
flog it
or frag it
they could
stab it
shoot it
shock it
or skin it
they could
drown it
dissolve it
dilute it
or drain it

but all they
ever do
is crush it

is there a single deity
with creativity
or have they all grown
as bored as me

my double

when my double crossed over
from another dimension
he didn't face immediate arrest
or indefinite detention
    instead I took in my other with open arms
    almost embracing him as a brother
    it was a mistake with consequences so great
    I wouldn't need to make another
my family and all of my friends
were quite apprehensive at first
but after a bit of my encouragement
everyone stopped assuming the worst
    they even grew to like the guy
    which made me kind of jealous
    he was better than me at everything
    and so unrelentingly overzealous
when news came that the portal was closing
and we both couldn't stay in the same reality
I feigned that I was feeling sadness
but deep down all I felt was glee
    when I saw him being pursued
    by a crowd of everyone I held dear
    under the fire of their torches
    I could almost taste my imposter's fear
it was then that it occurred to me
a truth so stark and grim
the mob was actually mine to deal with
because they were being led by him

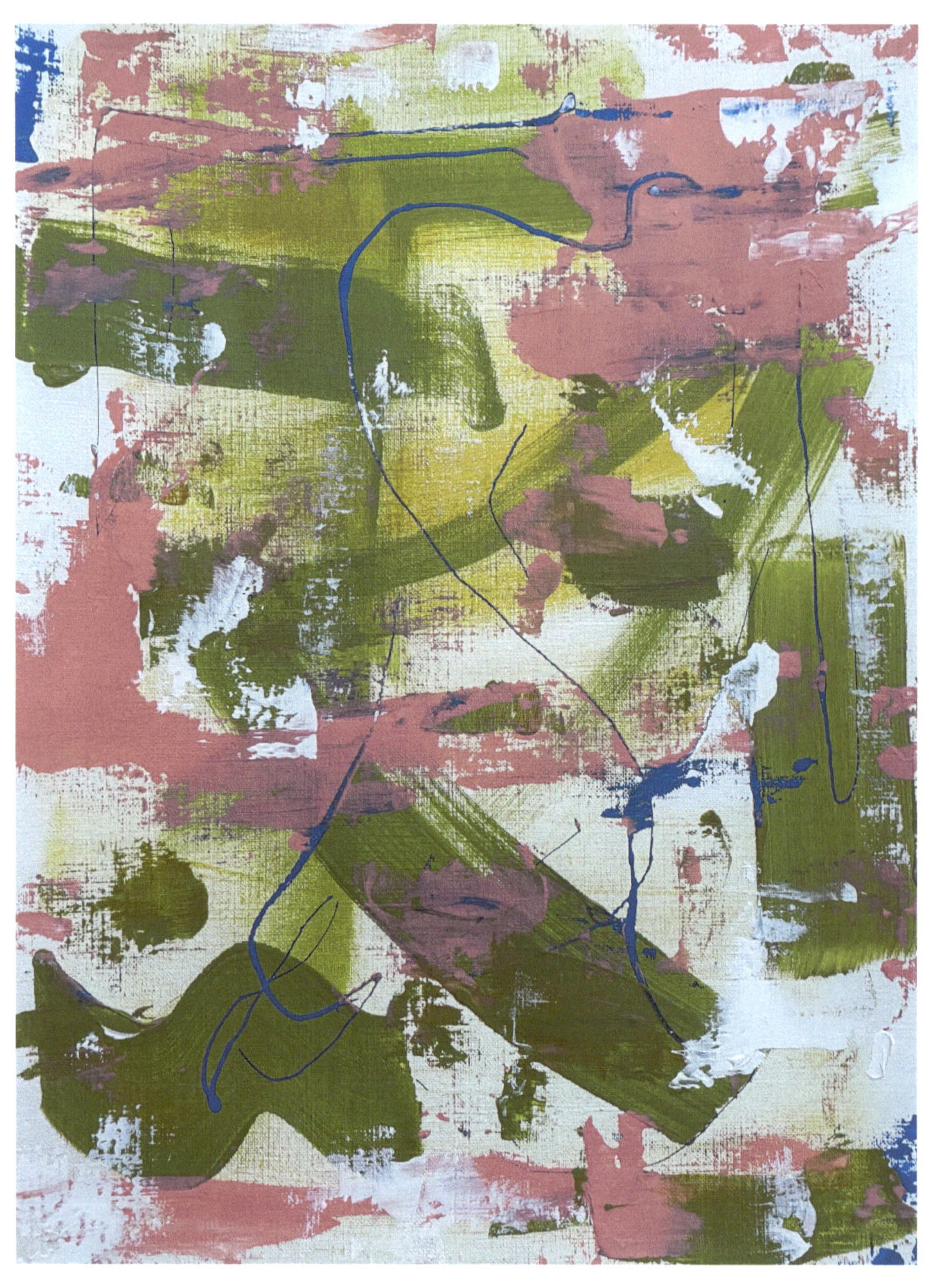

the moth

I am the moth   I am the light
&
I am drawn to the calm chaos of never

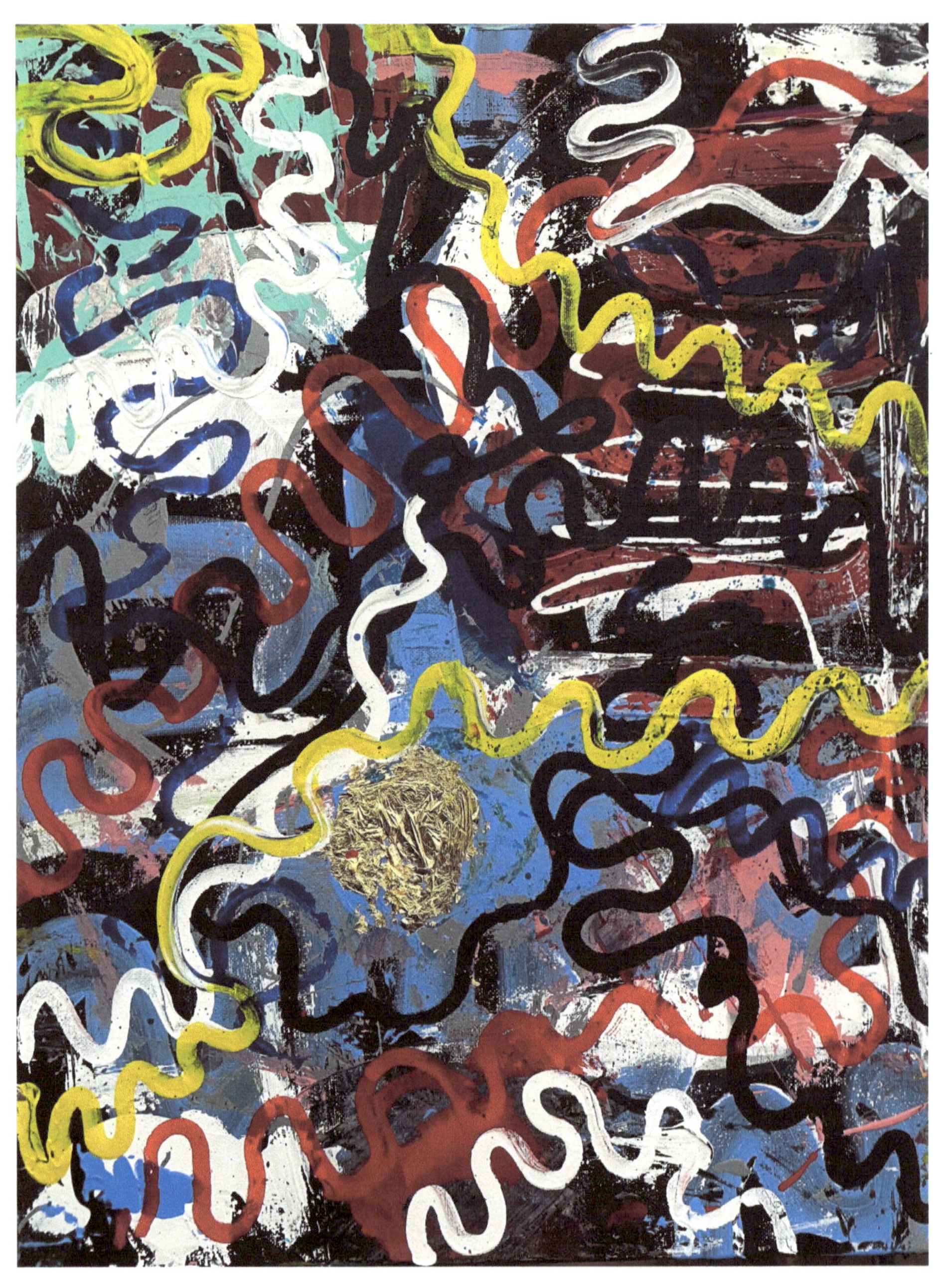

discarded dreams

you found me beside a pile
of discarded dreams
and you taught me
they still had a purpose
if I dug deep enough
to discover a seed
a better version of me
would resurface

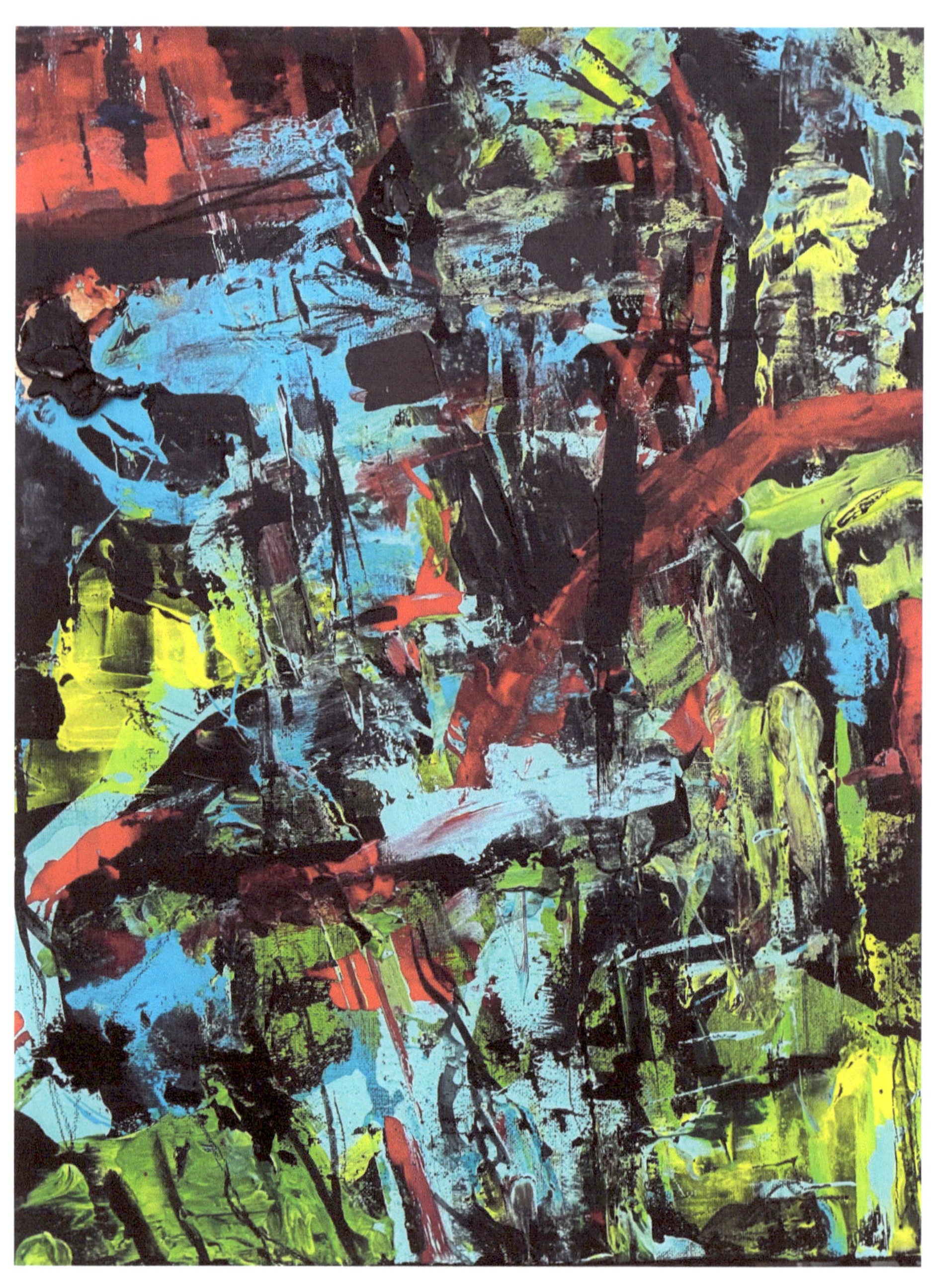

the flame

I am
the flame
that yearns
to burn
your wick
w
a
x
will drip

t
w h
e g
n i
l
will emit

and the day

will
be
reborn

between your thighs

lock m
we eyes e
as and l
t

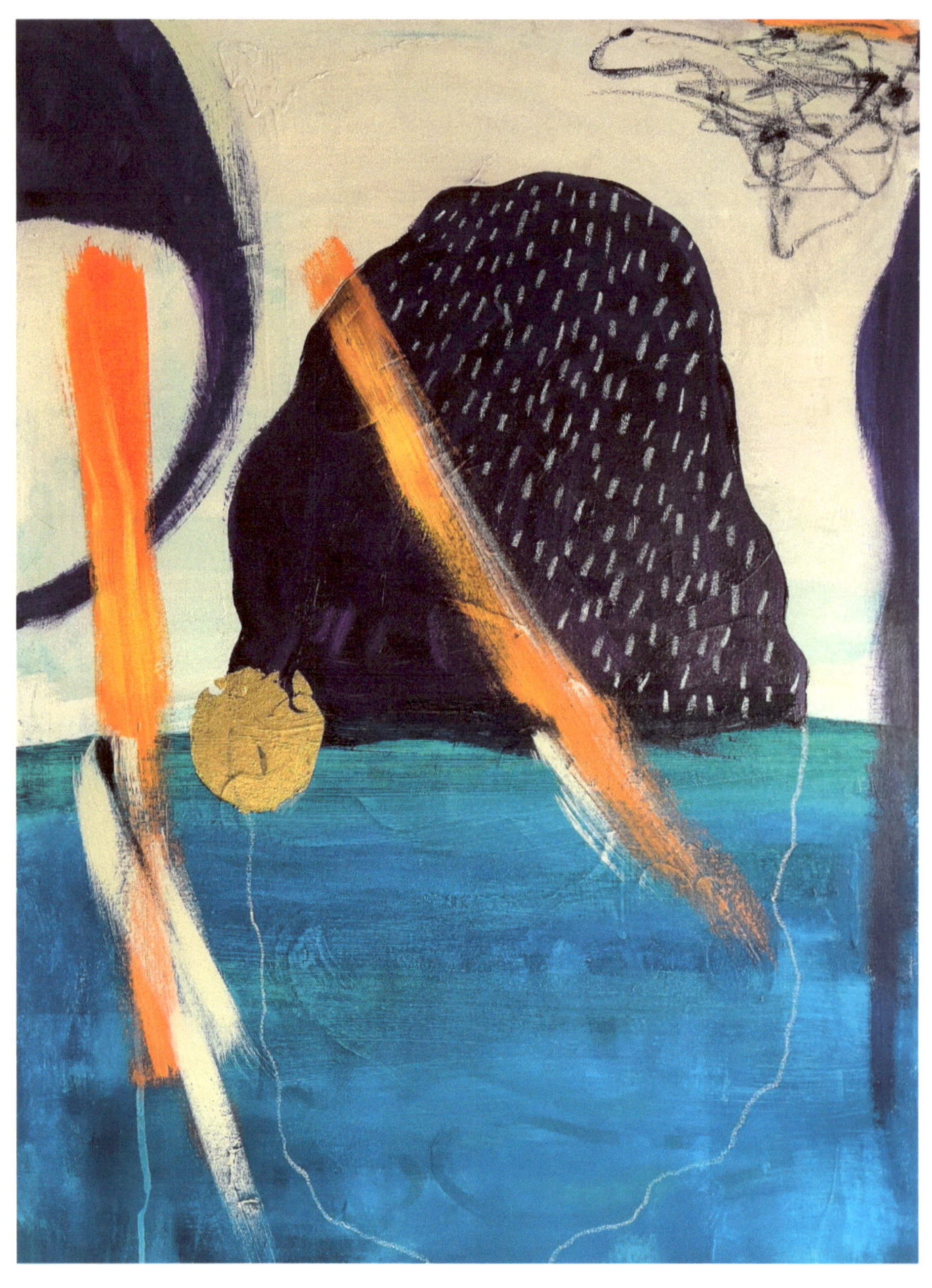

decadence

the steady drip
of decadence
has
flooded
our souls
poisoned
our mirrors
and
transformed
our bodies
into
prisons
our
visions
become
vestiges
as we hack away
at the root of self
our
hope
becomes
malice
as we bruise
even our best intentions
and
the
ideal
can't
be
reached
only
                gestured towards

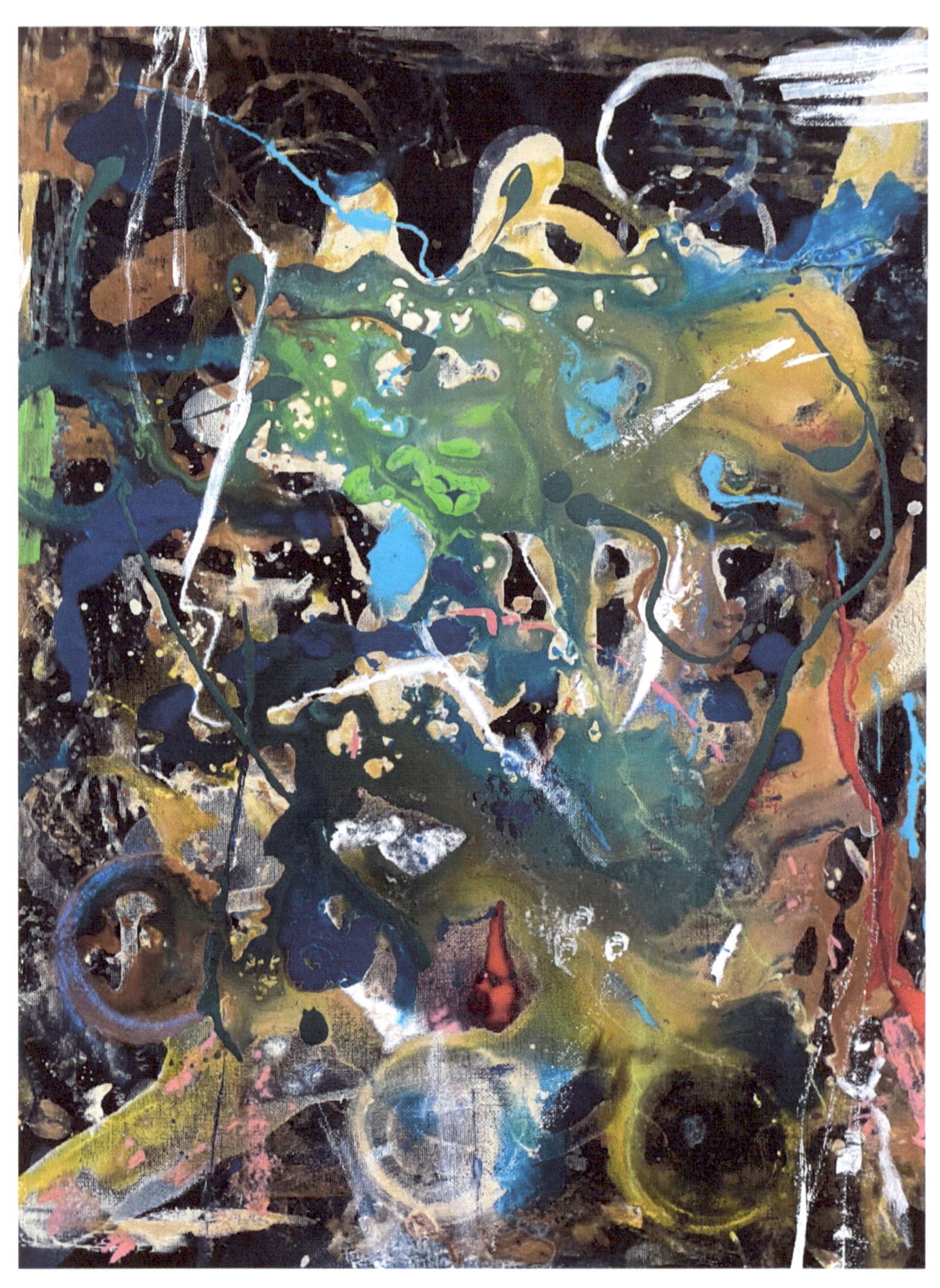

one hand on the wheel

like an out-of-body experience
cancelled halfway through
life still unfolds before my eyes
but the feelings fled the coop
pleasure pain and everything in between
now arrive with a clinical detachment
I label and seal them in mental compartments
hoping one day for more vivid reenactments
but for now I'm spectating from the driver's seat
if the road throws me a curve I may take a spill
I'm not asking for a destination or even a map
just a reason to keep one hand on the wheel

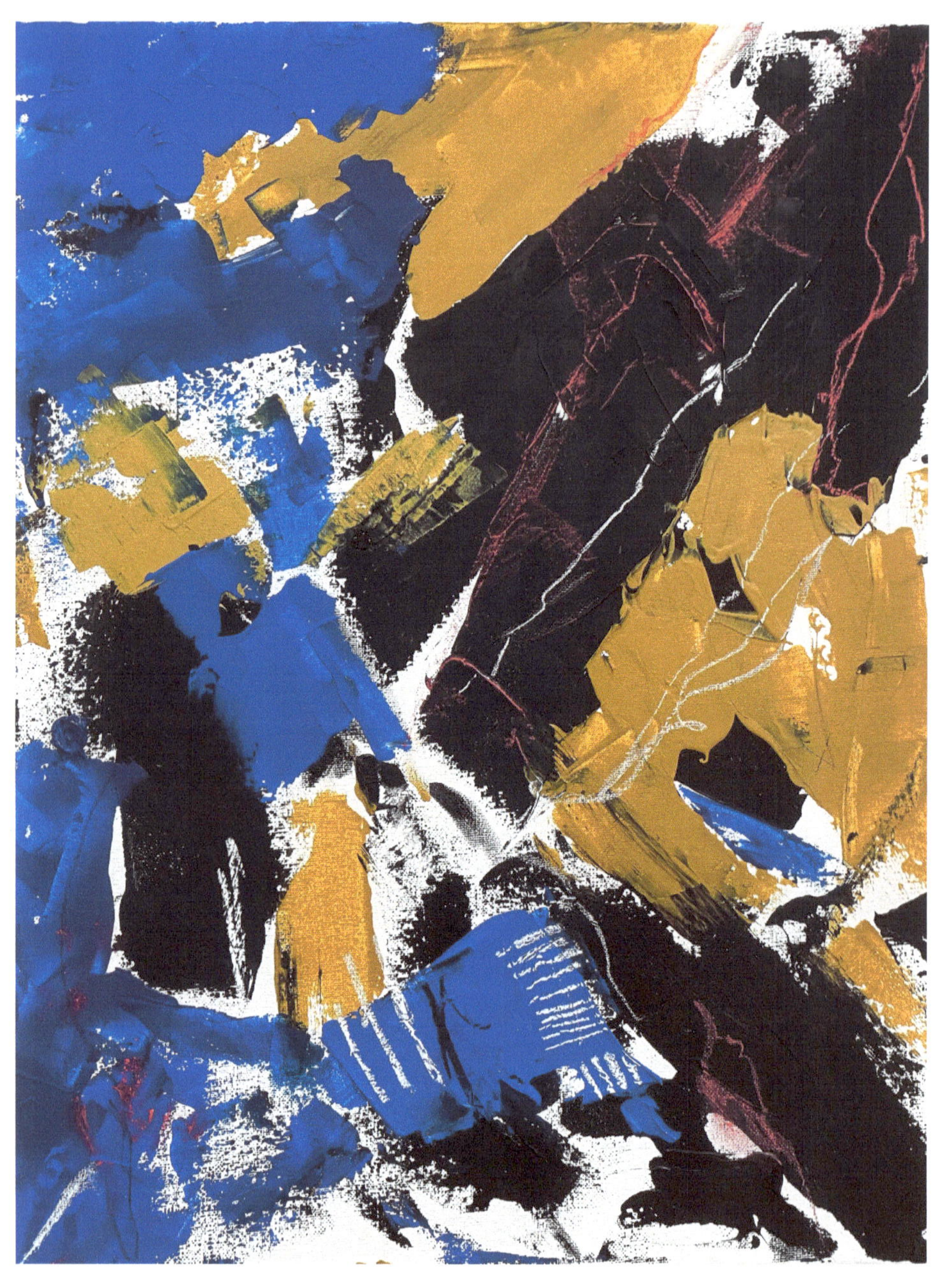

into the cracks

I took the parts of myself
that couldn't be comfortably worn
and I locked them outside
during the wildest of storms
but despite my defiance
wind wouldn't make them scatter
the rain joined them in alliance
and in the gutter they would regather
only to return unexpectedly
soaking into the cracks of my foundation
until I found that my life's rotation
had been disrupted by the gradual deflation
and I veered off course
swerving away from my identity
when it was revealed that I was the one
carving obscenities in my serenity
heading toward a destination
that had been rendered unclear
by a fog appearing everywhere
except for the mirrors

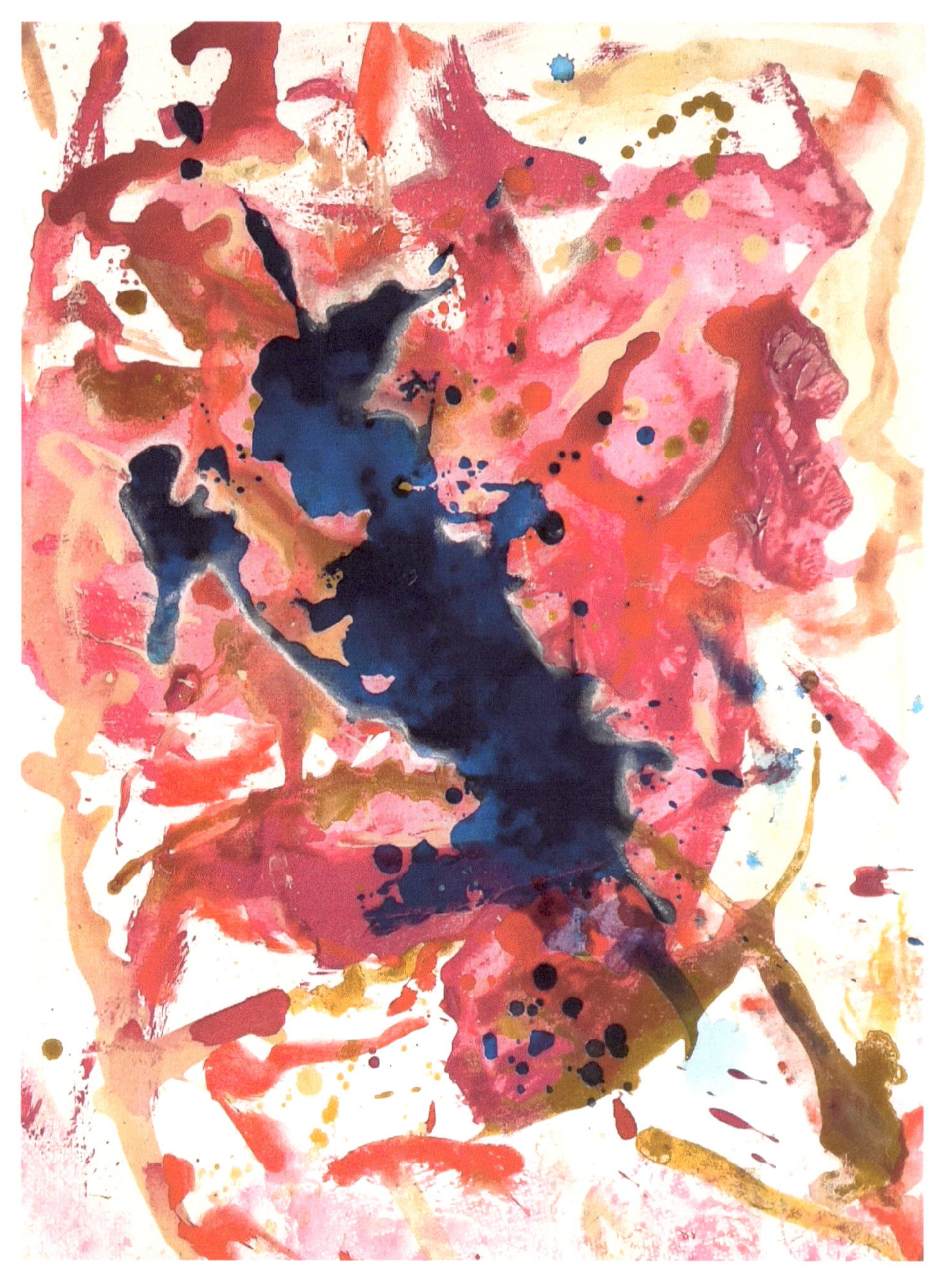

it belongs to you now

whoever is holding my heart hostage
please remember to keep it on ice
here's a list of all its food allergies
and don't forget it takes this medication twice
I'll put the supplies in an inconspicuous bag
and I'll leave it where your letter asked
but I'm not going to include any ransom money
because I honestly don't want it back

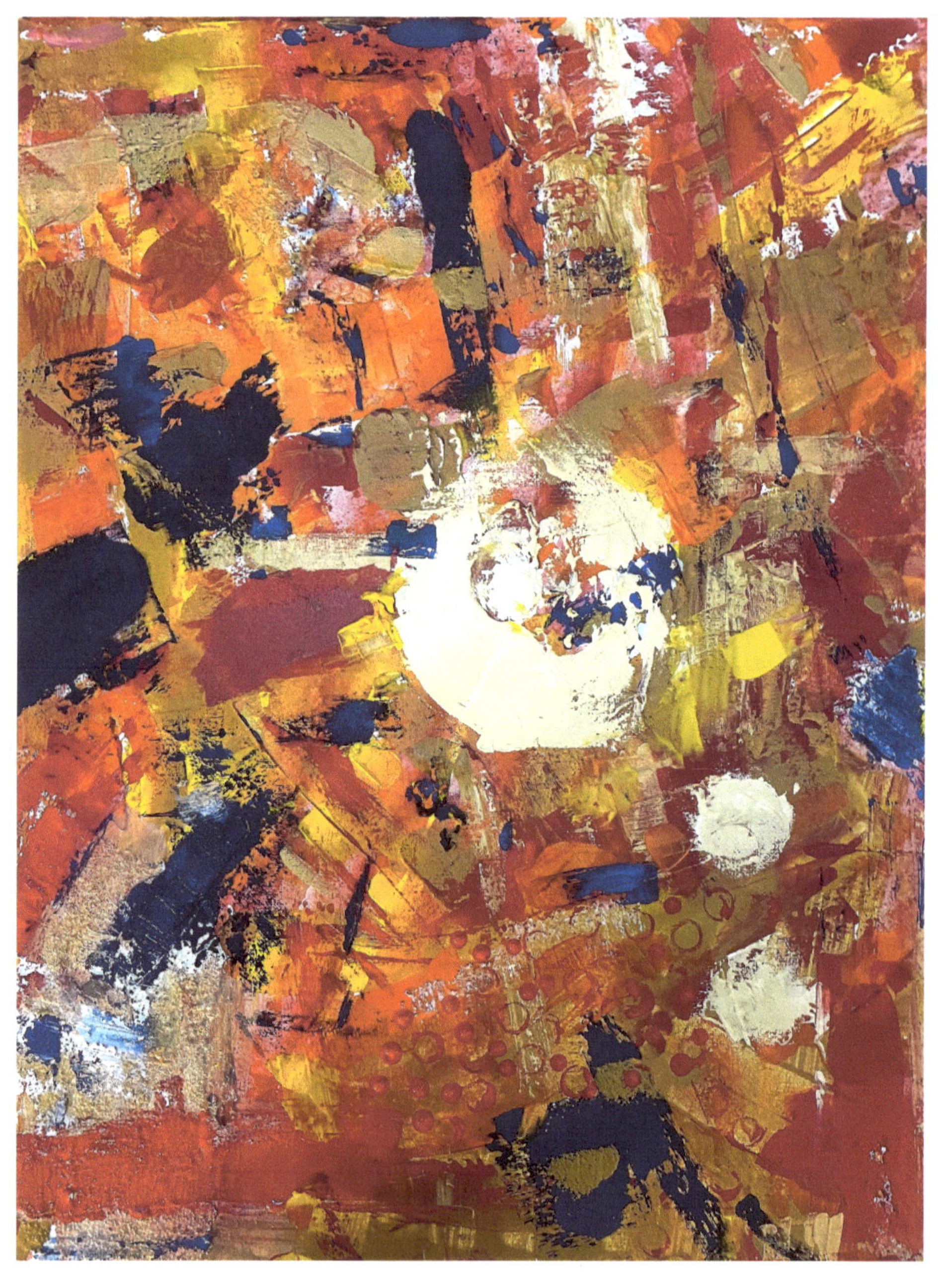

bad intentions

I told the sunrise about the sunset

I had bad intentions

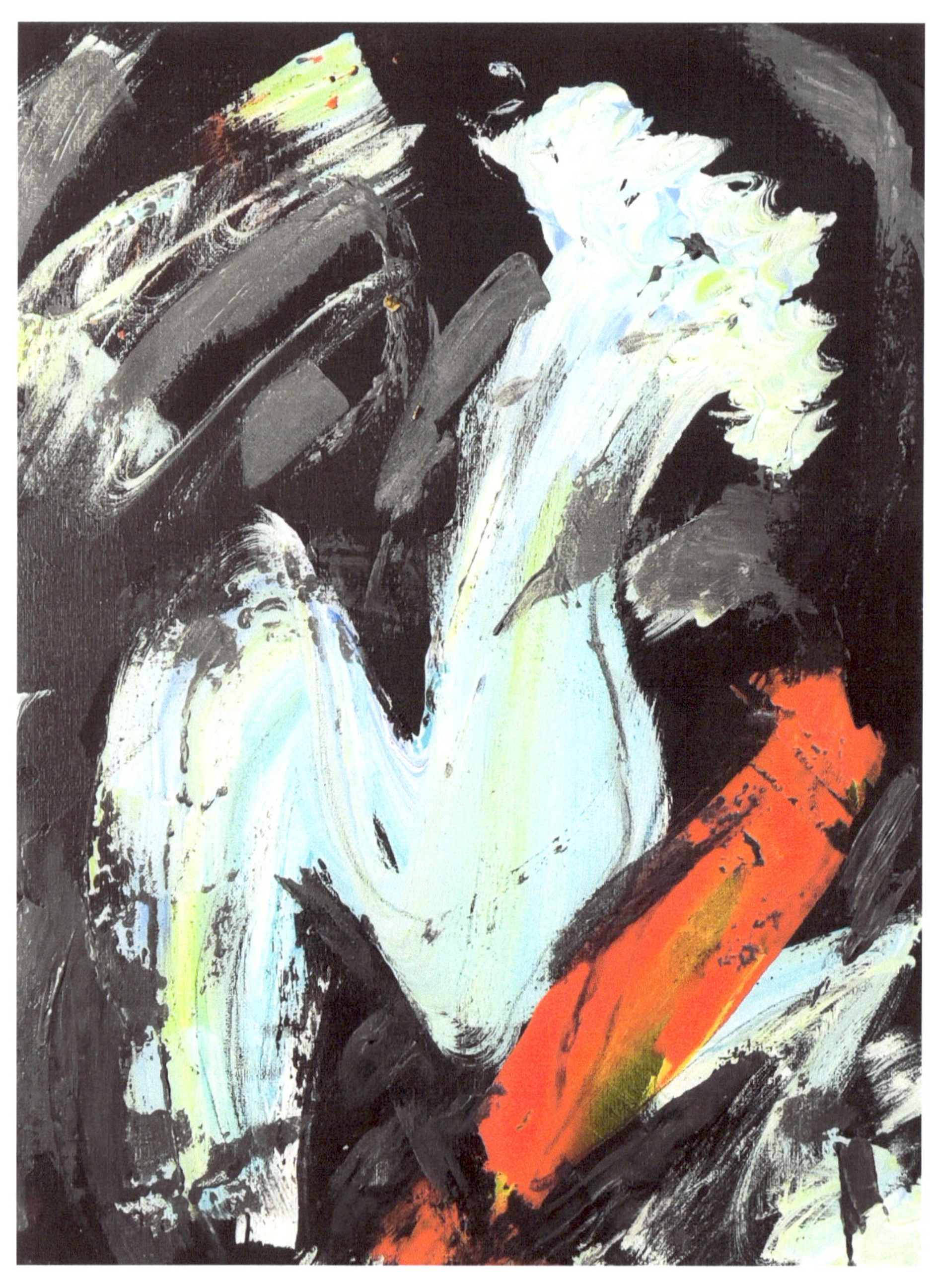

the hidden word

if the word decides to hide

behind the cloak of night

the writer must adjust to darkness

instead of turning on the light

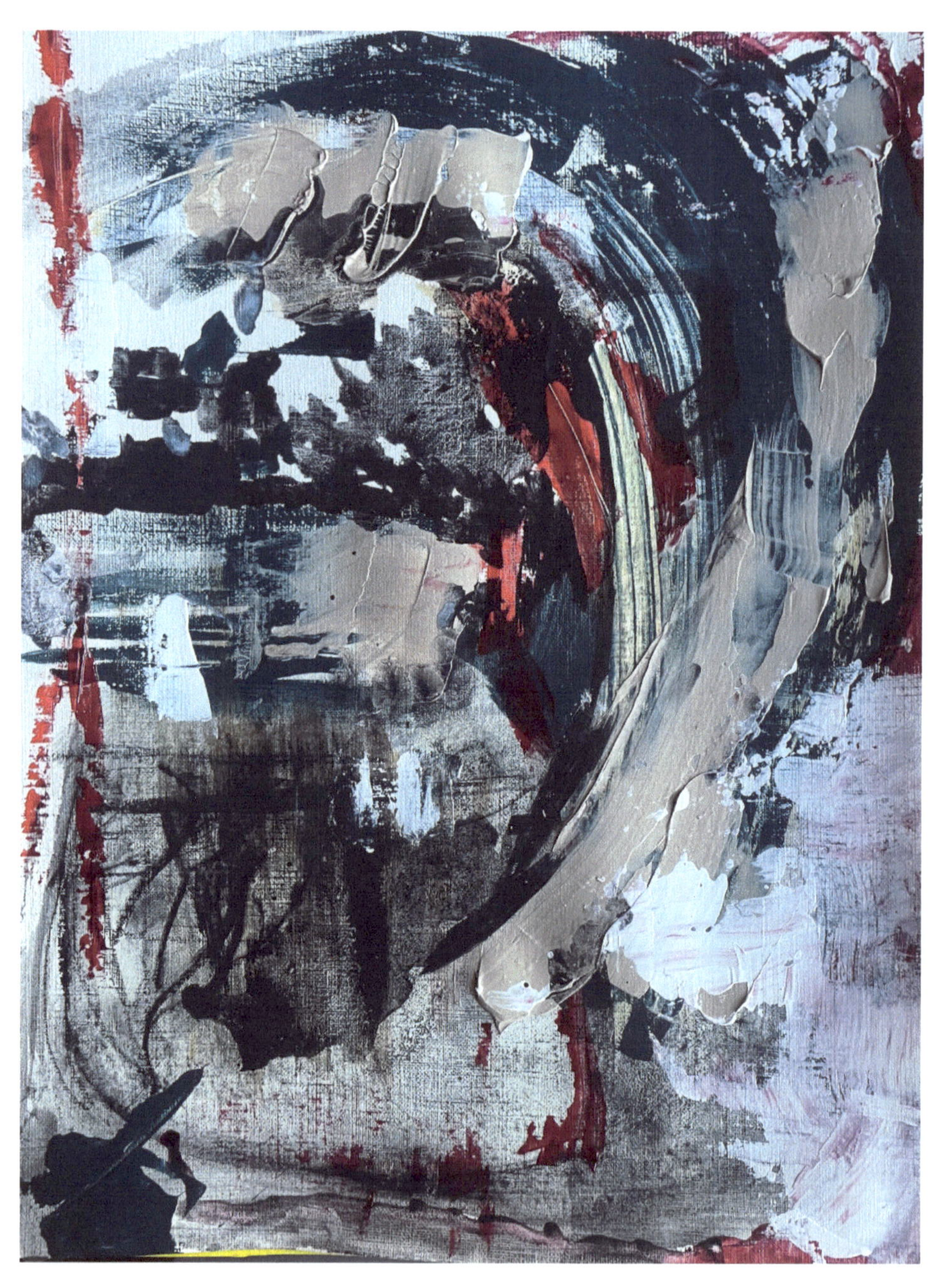

the swimmer and the shark

drawn

I am the swimmer to

~~~~~~~~~~~~~~~~~~~~~~~~~~~~~~~~my~~~~~~~~~~~~~~~~

and I am the shark own

blood
~~~~~~~~~~~~~~~~~~~~~~~~~~~~~~~~

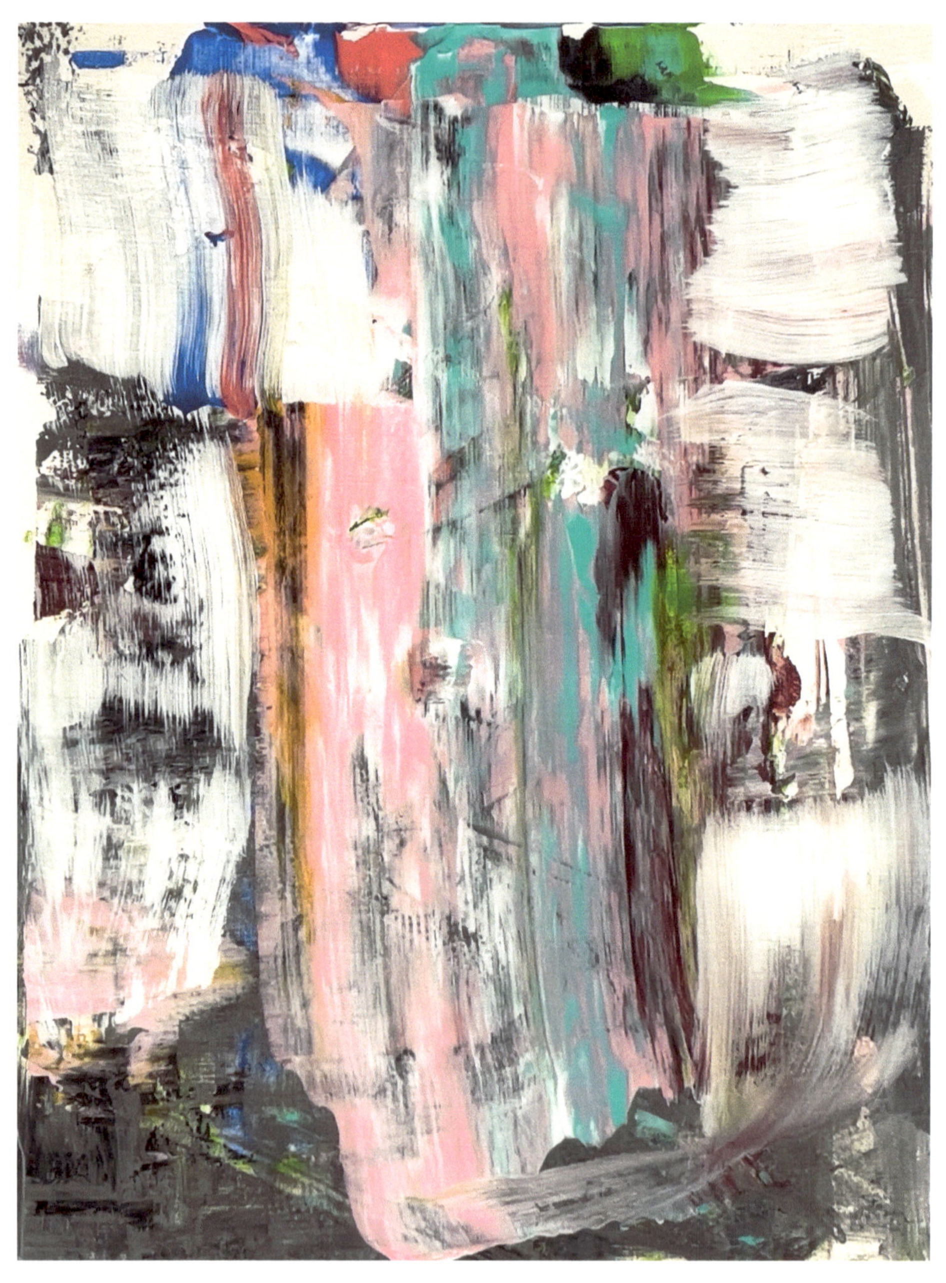

belief

something
in
believing I
tried even
I tried
tried believing
believing in
in myself
nothing

each one led
to the same
desolation
I think I ought
to put belief

back on the shelf

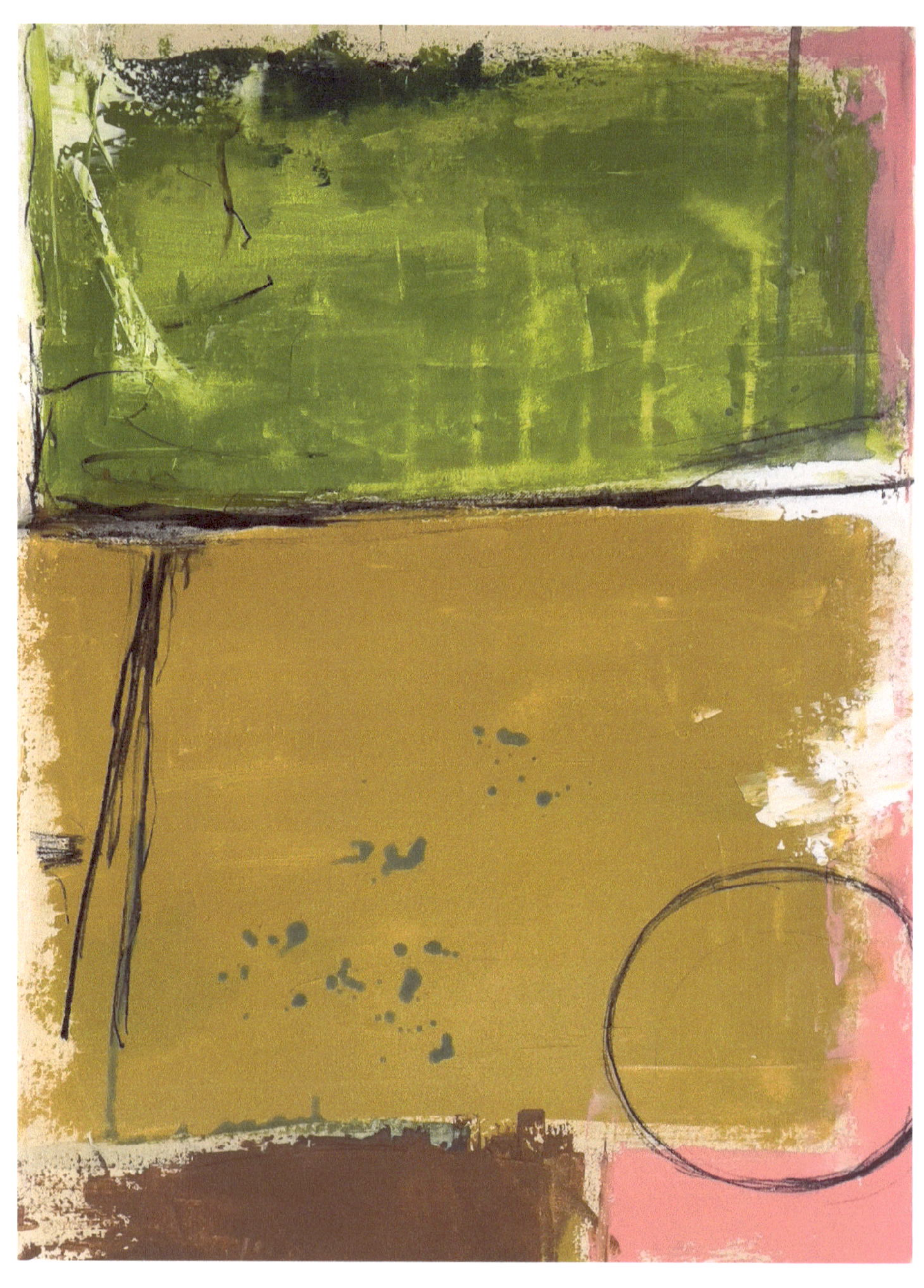

the recipe

the pendulum swings far too close
to those standing on the edge of time's coast
and the mountains will always begin to shift
just as you start to peer over love's cliff
sometimes you'll even make the mistake
of setting your incubator to incinerate
but when you finally get the recipe right
the scent will guide you through the darkest of nights
to do things you didn't think you were capable of
to reflect to reshape to grow and to love

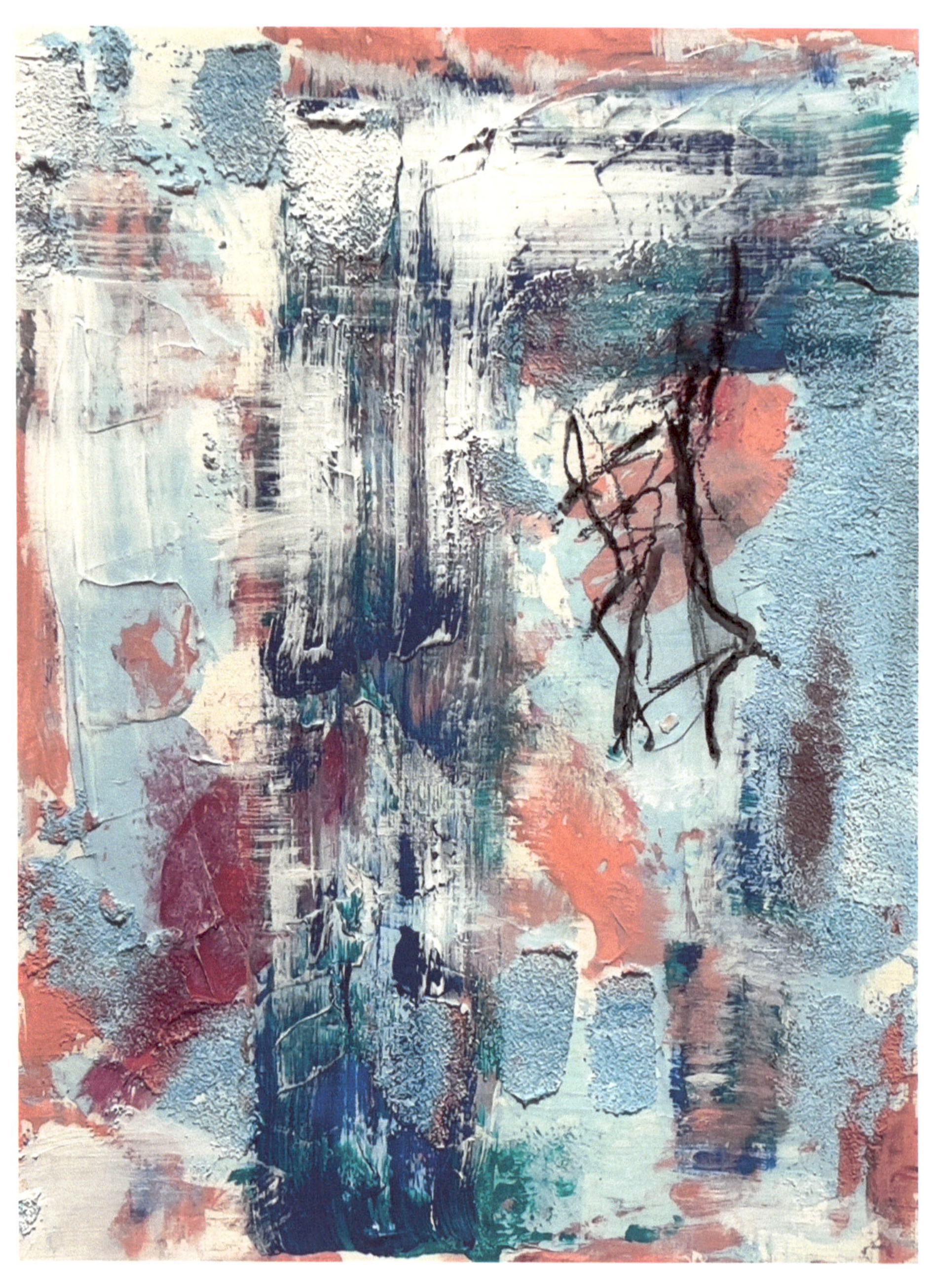

exploration

I found while I
undiscovered gazed into
planets your eyes
I thighs
charted your
out between
their journeying
surfaces

hovering over your atmosphere
I the of
followed source your sighs
and
I
landed
in
your crater
deepest

where
we
absorbed
the
stars
and
lit
up
the
skies

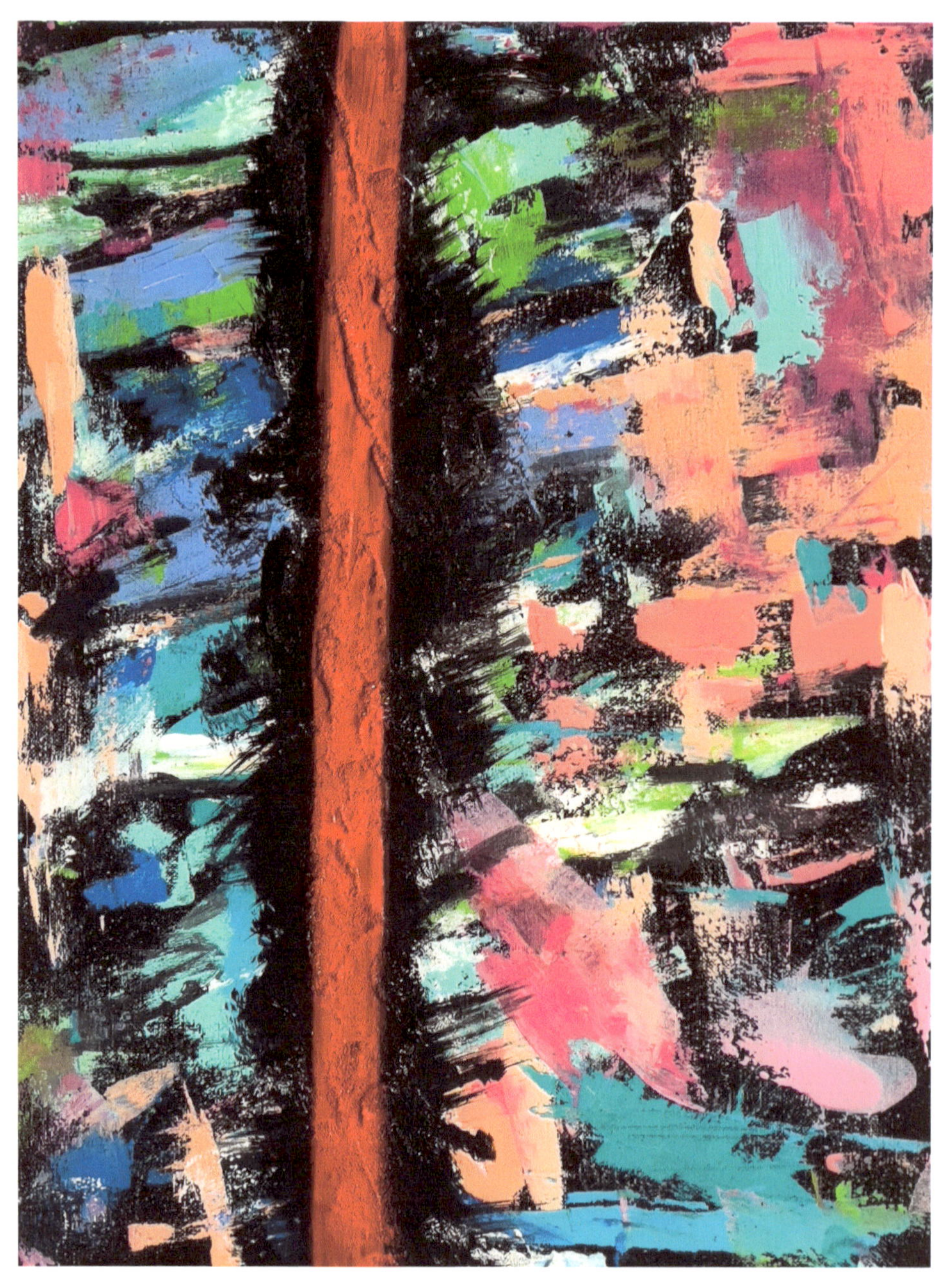

ricochet

another victim of ricochet

he shot for the stars

but it went through his brain

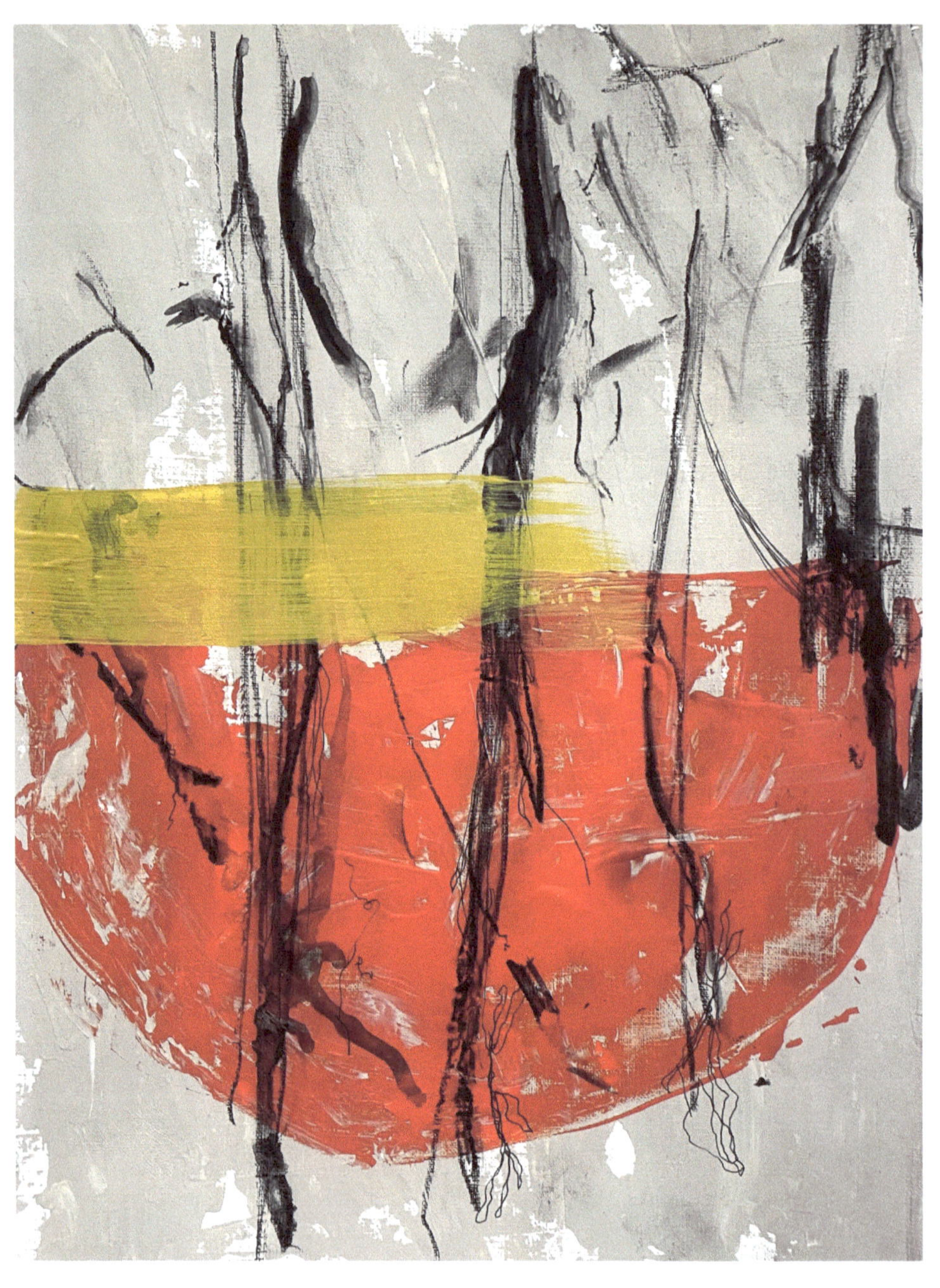

calculating infinity

the pain didn't fade

it
just
knew
which
pathways
to
evade

and now it's calculating infinity

in
the
unlit
alleys
of
my
brain

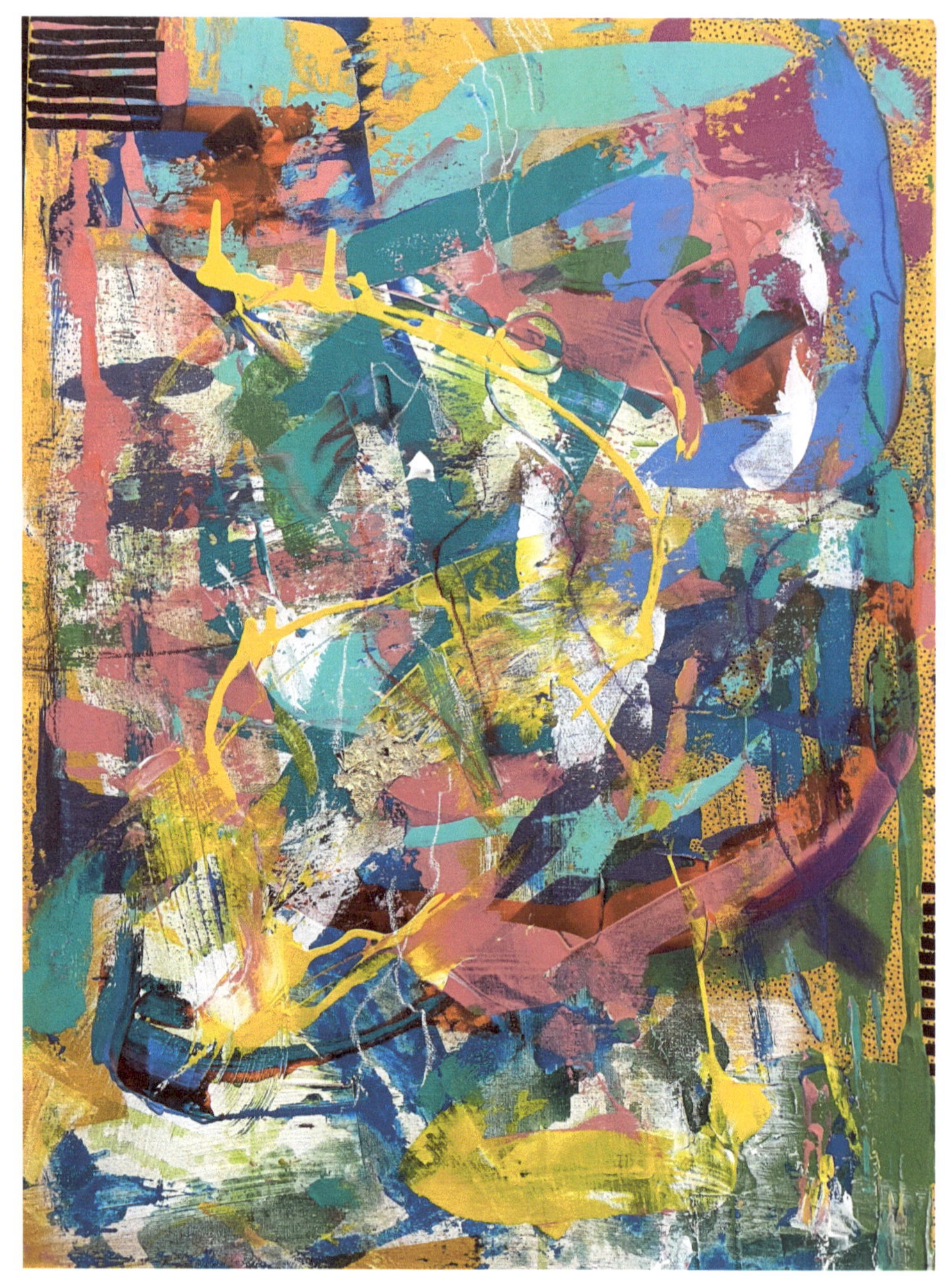

the healer

selflessness is at the core
of everything you do
healing with your heart and hands
even while feeling so blue
is there a way to believe in angels
without believing all the rest
because you lift people beyond the heavens
to this I can attest

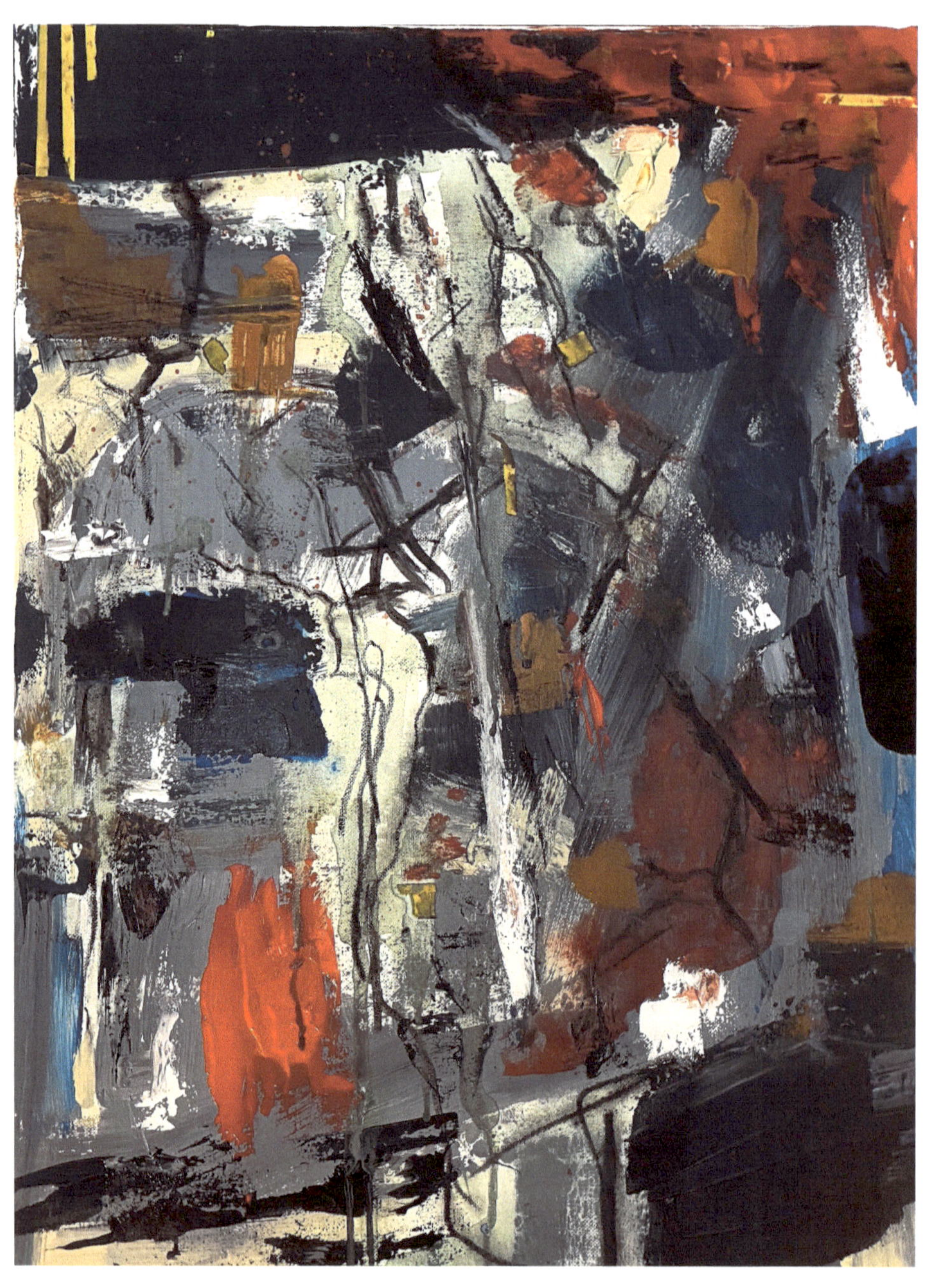

a twenty-year heist

it was a twenty-year heist
without a getaway vehicle
they promised overnight wars
but released six thousand sequels

and they acted as though their desires
to dice up an entire region
started the day the towers fell
but their own words can trace their treason

for decades they signed their letters
pushing for "securing strategic interests"
but we knew exactly what they were saying
and still it didn't make any difference

of course they'll never see their day
facing trial at the Hague
because the blood that soaked their money
somehow doesn't bleed through the flag

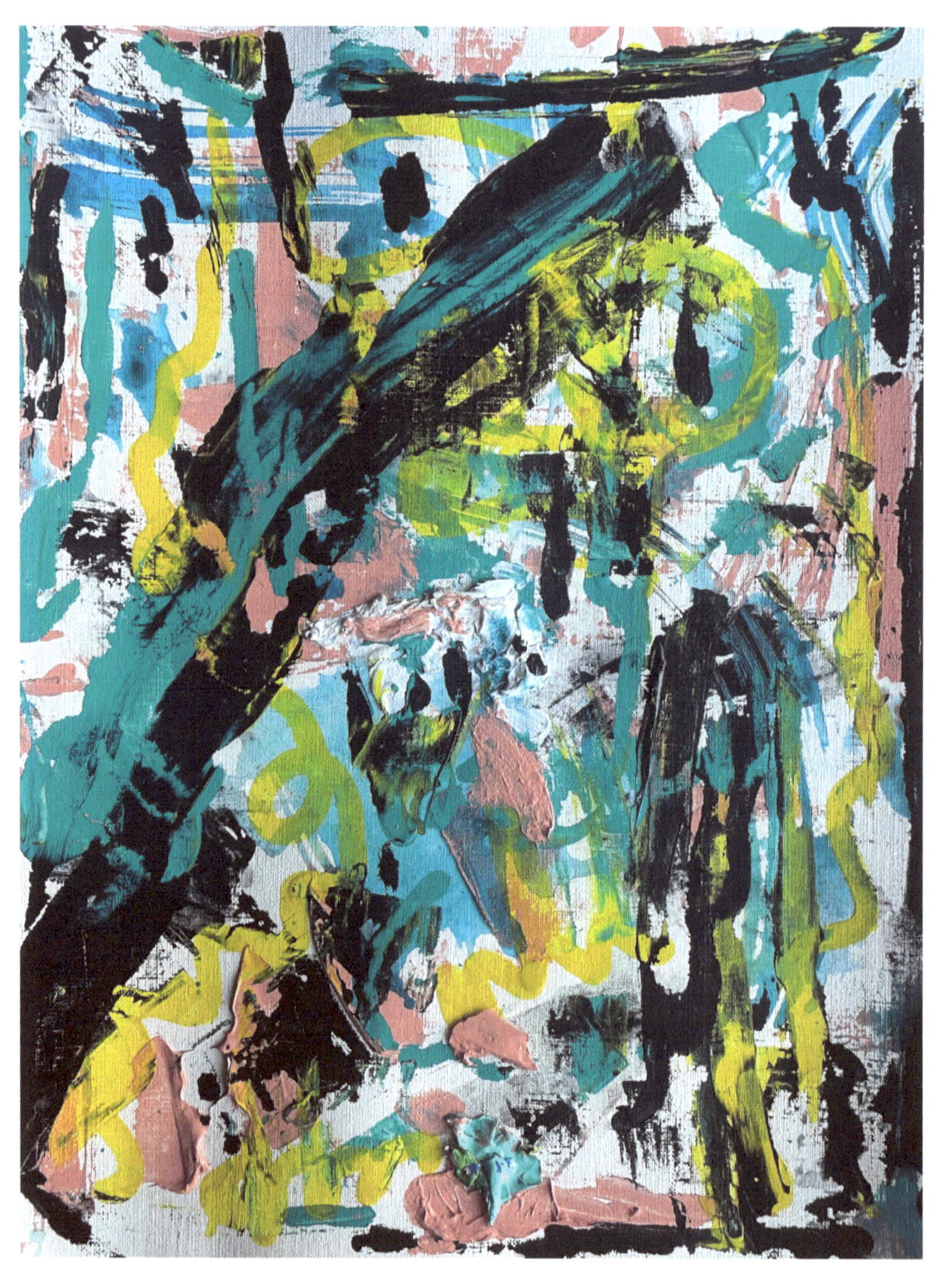

magic show

when we meet
there will be magic
if I can get my rabbit
to come out of the hat
you can wiggle my wand
and I'll shuffle your deck
as long as you promise
not to saw me in half

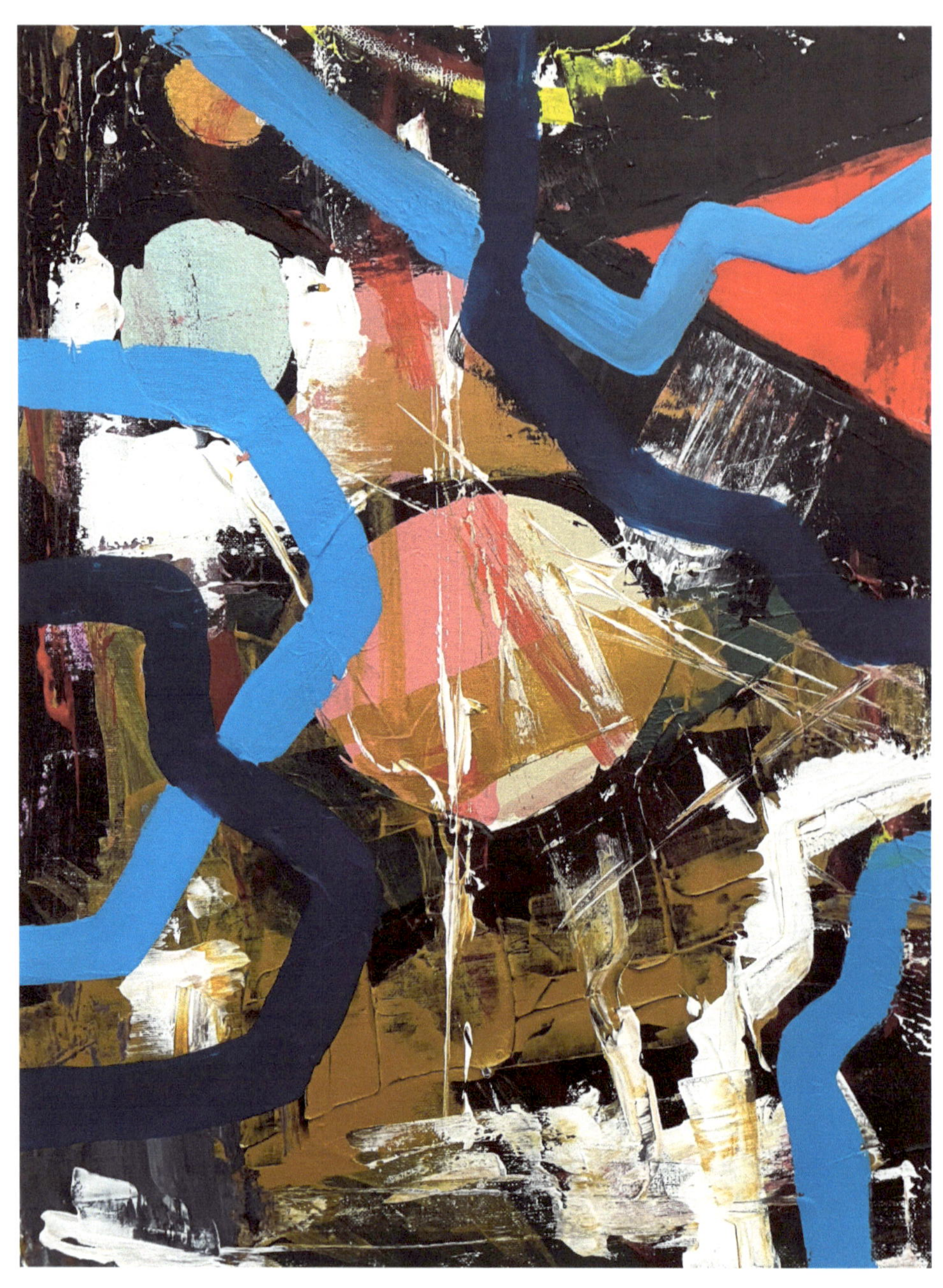

heaven and hell

when a FOIA request
put their hustle to rest
god and the devil fled the scene
a major bombshell
revealed heaven and hell
had been populated randomly
most of the angels retired or quit
christ came back throwing a televised fit
and as a result even he was sent below
now that mother theresa and charles manson
are in the same wing of the eternal mansion
what you reap has very little to do with what you sow

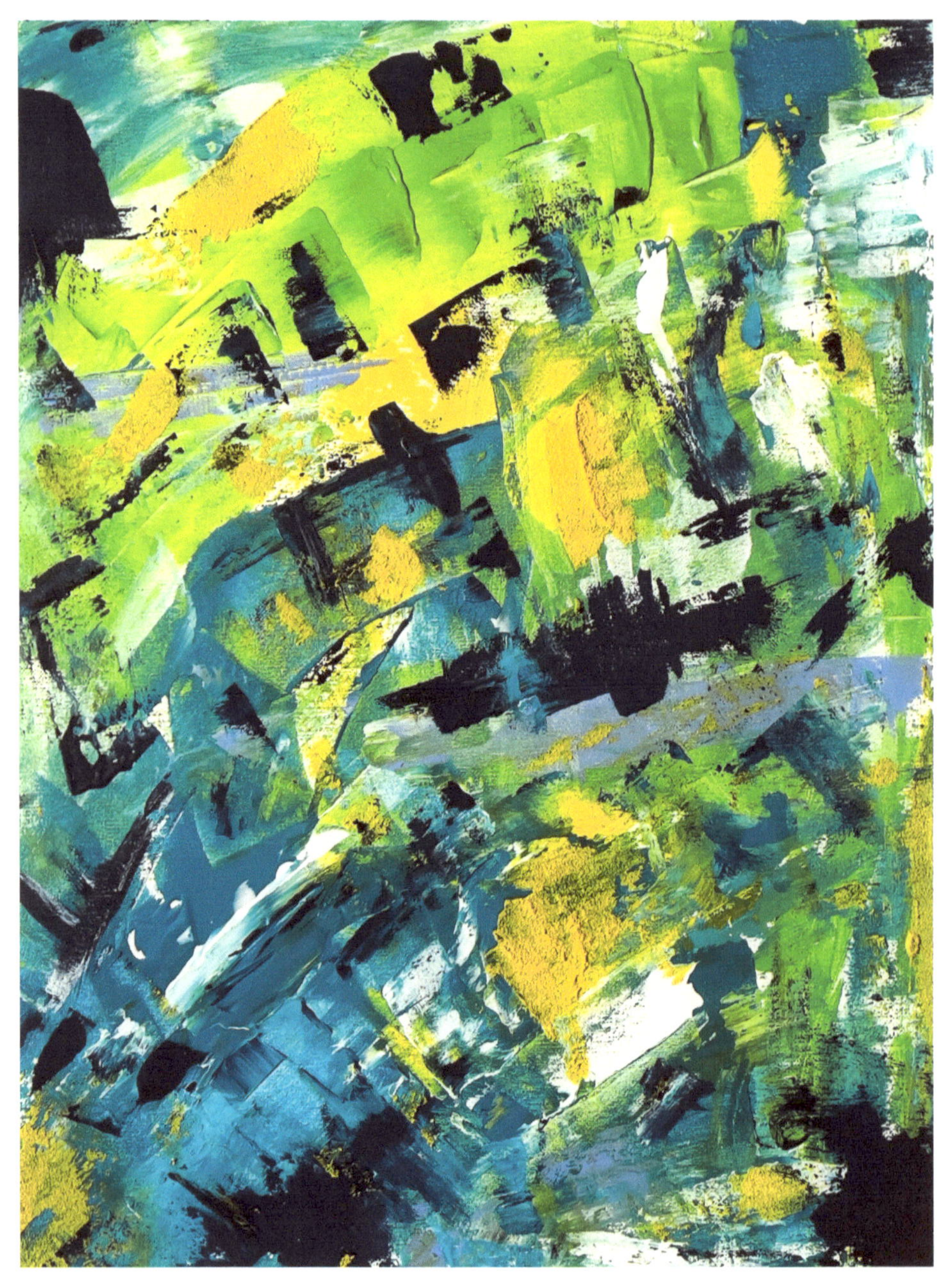

too bright

{ }

{ }

{ }

I'm not sure if
I shine too bright
for this world or if this
world shines too bright
for me but the one thing I
can tell you without any
hesitation is there's a
whole lot of shining
| and not enough
| being seen
|
|
|
|
|
|
¤

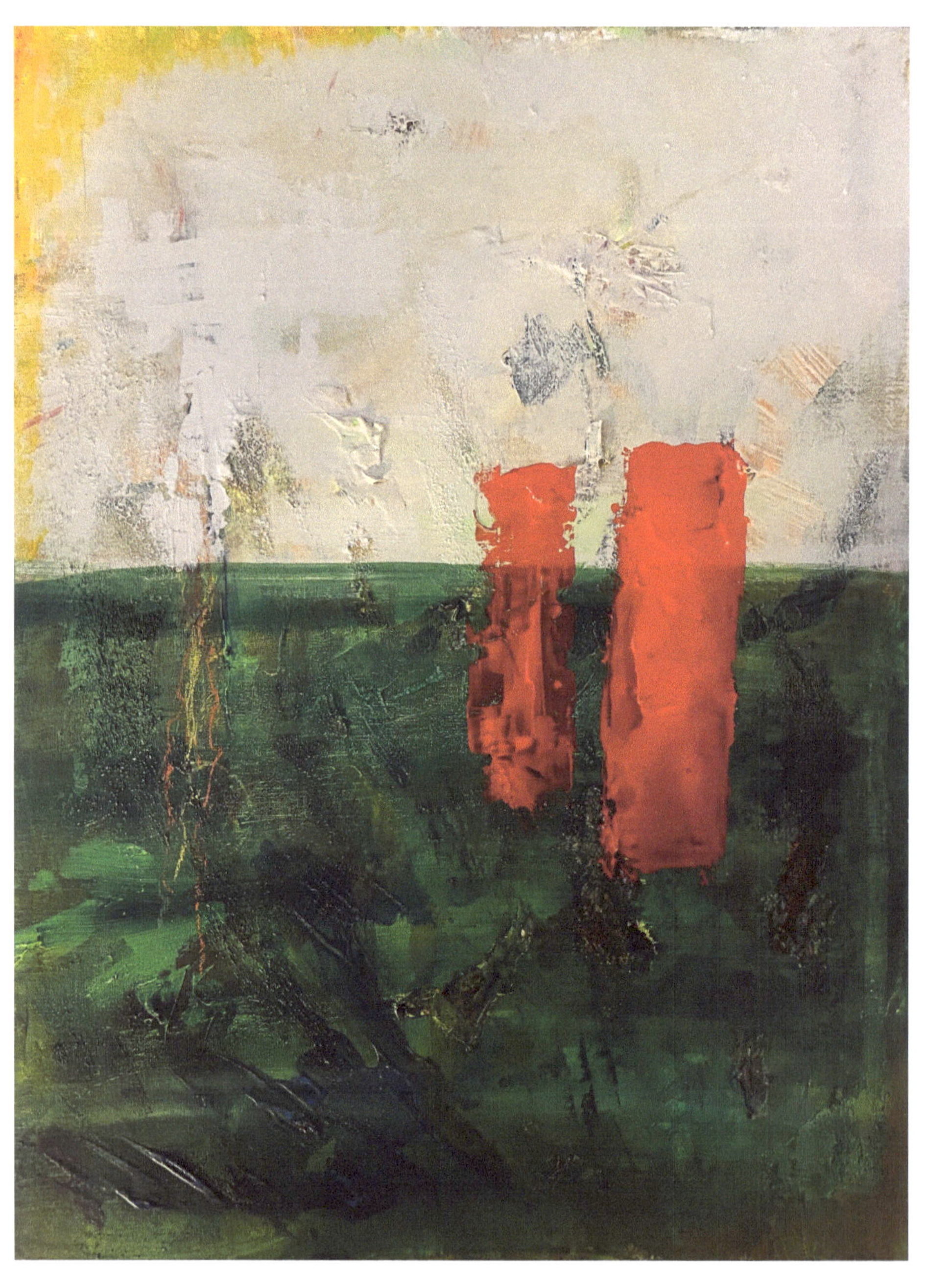

on second thought

I'd write
a novel
but I'd
kill off
all the
characters
thirty
pages in
and
we'd be
left with
a dozen
chapters
of
wind
whistling
through
bloodstained
grass

maybe
it's time
I wrote
a novel

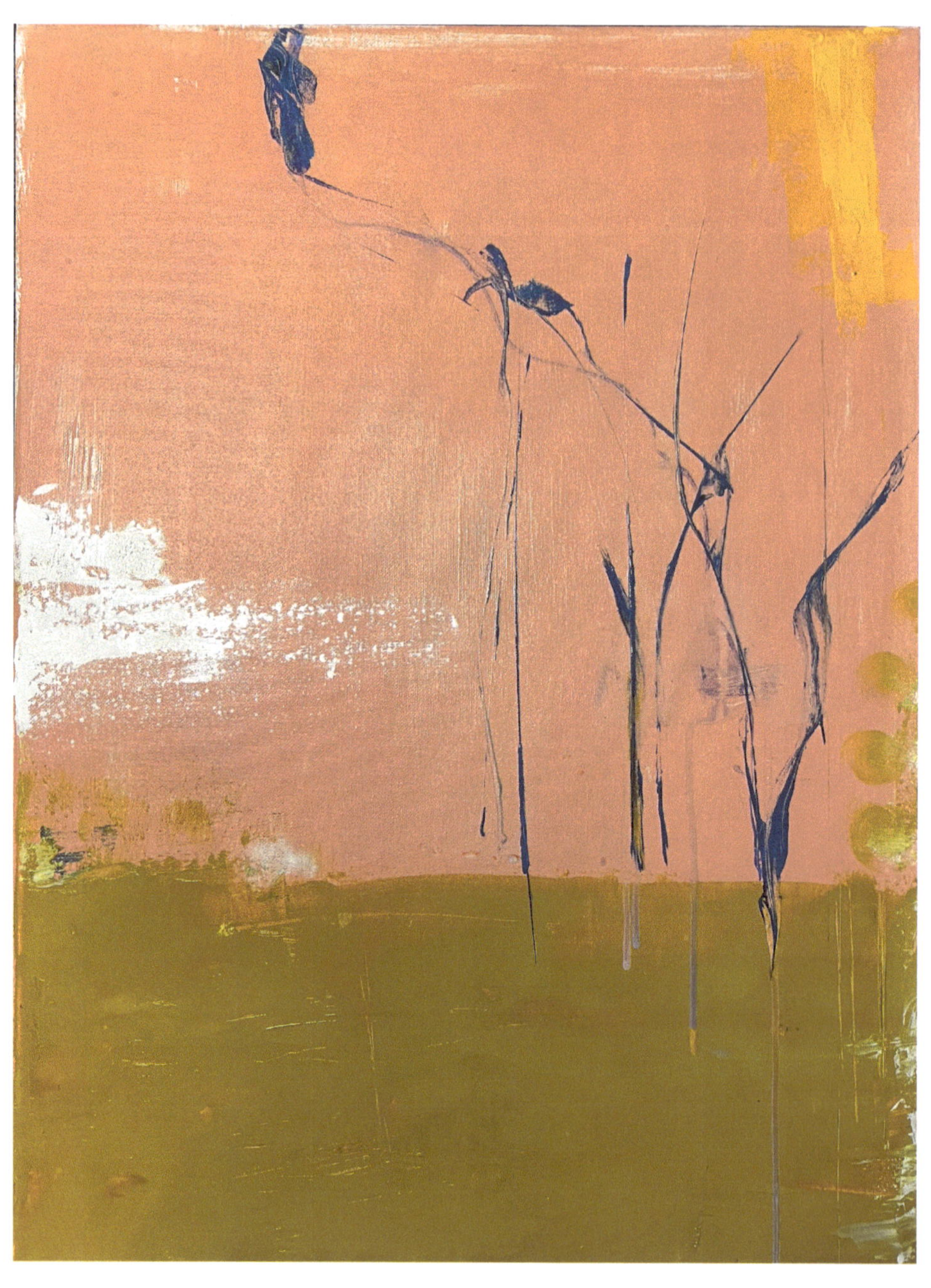

a finale

this seems like a finale
all my plot points are wrapping up
and with the backdrop of a burning sky
I can't even pretend that it feels abrupt

my show never found an audience
though it ran for years
it ran from my dreams and toward my doubts
racing side by side with my fears

maybe we'll get renewed by another network
or find ourselves revived through syndication
but the next time you find my credits rolling
assume my critics finally got their vindication

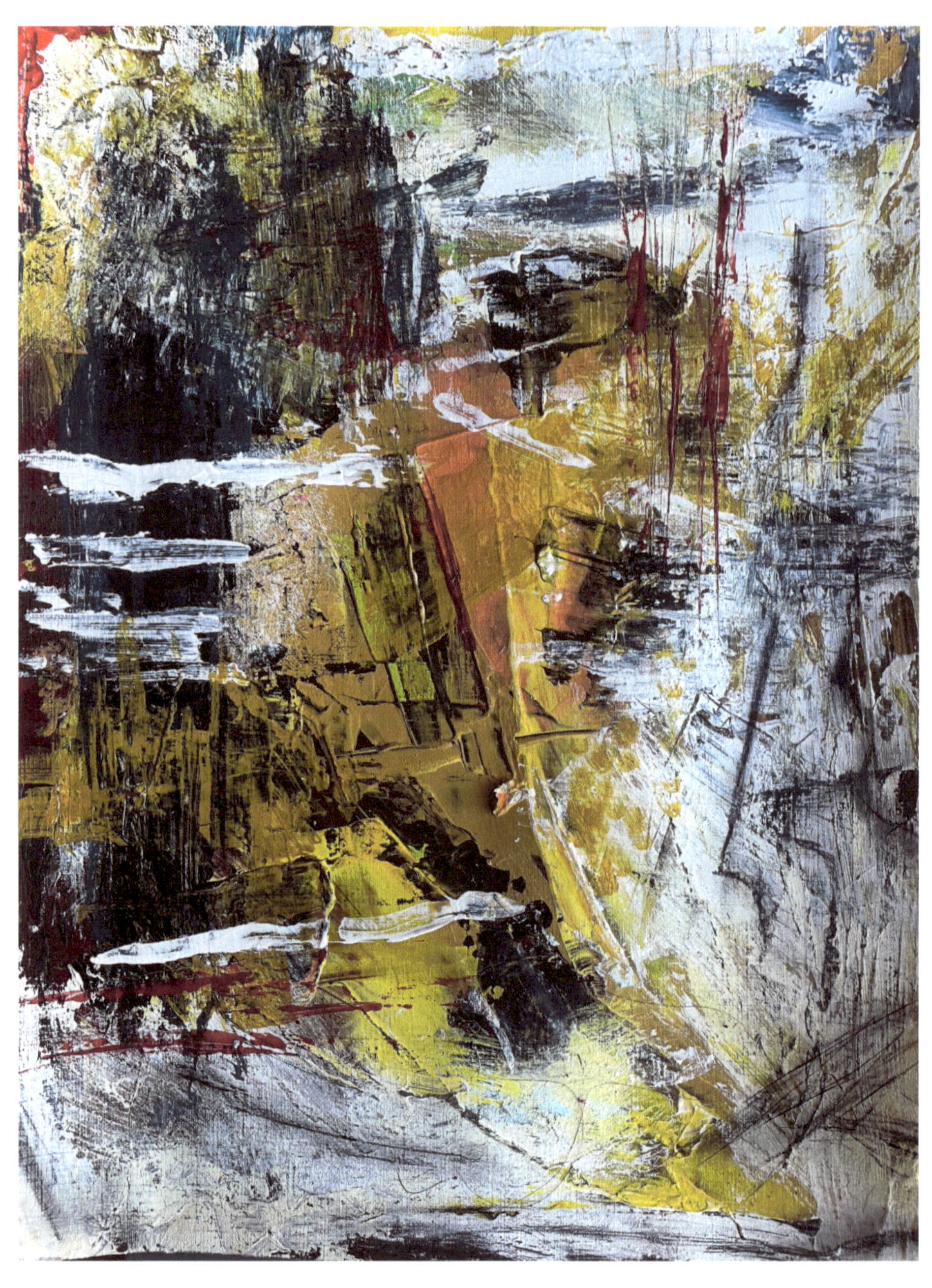

the song of surrender

while the song of surrender
sounds so sweet
to sing it would lift you
straight up off your feet
and the music wouldn't end
until after your final breath
because the song of surrender
only plays in the key of death
sometimes I hear it faintly
like it's tuning its instruments to me
but I somehow decline the offer to duet
knowing I can still find my own symphony

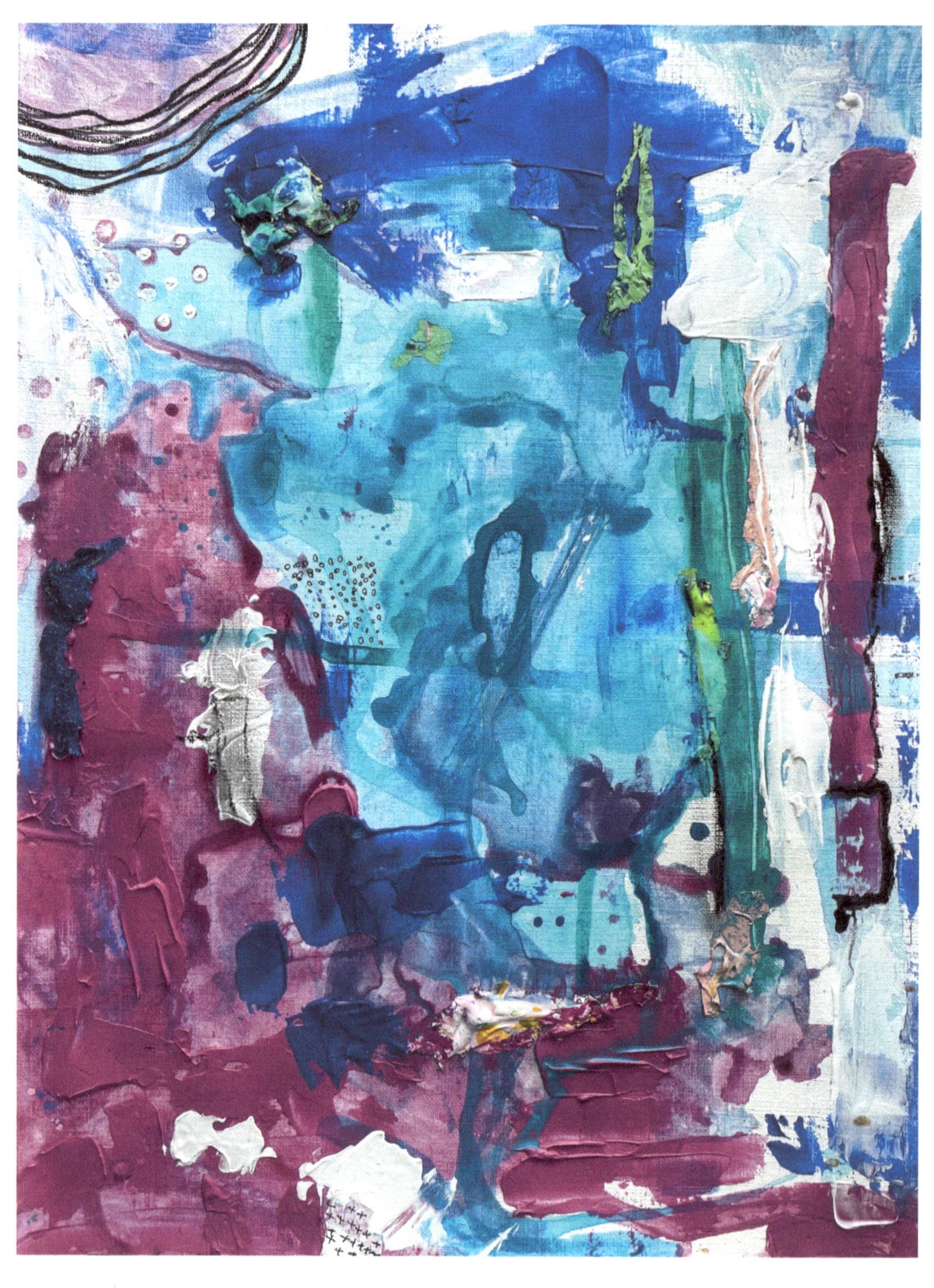

your turn

there is a poem in everyone
if you take the time to learn
          when to feed it
          when to bleed it &
          when to let it burn
                    then it will be your turn